EUROPE IN ARMS

By the Same Author

EUROPE

IN

ARMS

LIDDELL HART

RANDOM HOUSE · NEW YORK

FIRST PRINTING

Manufactured in the United States of America
By the Stratford Press, Inc., New York

Tribute from a Sassenach

to

IAN HAMILTON

and

JOHN KENNEDY

leaders of men

and men of imagination

Foreword

THE REARMAMENT OF EUROPE, AS WELL AS the technical development which affects it, is moving so fast that anyone who attempts to write a book on the subject is like a man trying to jump on a bus along a road that has no halting places. If he were to set out to write an entirely fresh book, allowing the time needed to study each aspect of the question, he would almost certainly have to rewrite it by the time he had finished it. In these circumstances, it has seemed best to make some use of material already written, after studies of the various problems, adding to this as required. The original material thus utilized consists partly of points from articles contributed to *The Times* during the past two years, as its Military Correspondent and adviser on defence in general; partly of points from articles contributed to various British and American reviews, military and general, or to *The New York Times*. They have been selected for their bearing on the general theme and on these foundations the book itself has been built up with new material. With more time a much better book could have been written on the subject. But for that it would be necessary to call a halt in the ever-accelerating process of rearmament and progress of invention. And the on-looker, although he may see most of the game, is not allowed a whistle.

In treating such a subject there are many aspects which call for attention and invite discussion. I realize that those covered here are by no means exhaustive. The arrangement, too, has been a difficulty because so many of the aspects blend into others. The idea which has guided the grouping ultimately adopted is made clear by the titles given to the four parts of the book; but these parts are not watertight compartments—they merely represent the predominant nature of the chapters in each. Thus the chapters in Part I are mainly concerned with the present state of the forces of the Great Powers; those in Part II with some of the chief problems of warfare and current defence policy; those in Part III with an analysis from different angles, and in the light of past experience, of the process of forecasting the nature, course, and effects of future wars. The opening chapter is a reminder of the purpose of defence, lest we forget that it is only a means to an end.

LIDDELL HART

on

SPAIN

---

*This chapter was received
by the publishers from Captain Hart after the book was
already off press.*

JULY 1937

Lessons from Spain

BECAUSE OF THE NATURAL FOG OF WAR IT HAS always been difficult to gauge the course of a campaign actually in progress, and it has become more difficult with the modern development of censorship and propaganda in creating artificial "smoke." The outline of military events in Spain has now, however, become clear enough to enable the distant observer to estimate the situation and the factors which have governed it. During the autumn and most of the winter a state of deadlock prevailed, hardened by the weather. During these months the Government forces as a whole remained on the defensive, and succeeded, despite their inferior equipment and training, in frustrating the Nationalists' efforts to extend their gains. With each month of continued successful resistance, the Government's prospects were the more likely to improve—so long, at any rate, as General Franco did not receive a great increase of assistance from foreign sources. The deadlock was broken by the fall of

Malaga, a Nationalist coup which was marked by good strategic judgment as well as by Italian backing on a new and important scale. The resistance was slight, its moral stability being easily shaken by the effect of surprise on a state of unpreparedness.

The effort had a significant moral reaction. The Government were spurred to change their strategy, and to attempt a widespread series of offensives. These, as was to be expected, made no great material impression, except on the casualty totals. As was also to be expected, the exhaustion of the attackers offered a more promising opportunity for the Nationalist forces to renew their offensive. It remained to be seen whether General Franco's forces were capable of exploiting it sufficiently under the conditions of modern warfare. Their most threatening effort was the three-pronged stroke from Siguenza south-westwards towards Guadalajara and Madrid, delivered on March 8. While it preserved the assets of surprise and mobility, its promise was high, but these waned all the sooner because of the intervention of General Mud, which gave the resistance time to harden and to be reinforced by General Miaja. Stuck in the mud, the Italians, who largely composed the attacking force, soon became ripe objects for a counterstroke, which came on March 13. Its dramatic success repeated the experience of the World War, where the most striking victories, so long as the forces were fairly well matched, were produced by action of the counter-offensive form. It also showed, as the Abyssinian War had shown previously, that aircraft are specially formidable in such action, and that their advent has greatly enhanced its power. In Abyssinia the Italians had been the demonstrators of this development; at Guadalajara they served as the body on which the demonstration was performed.

While this is a lesson, now amply attested, to which all those who are concerned with the creation of armies may well pay attention, we should curb the inclination to draw too detailed deductions of general application from particular episodes of the Spanish War. There are signs, for example, of a tendency to treat the Guadalajara offensive as a trial of mechanised forces and an exposure of their defects. Commentators have even described it as the first big battle in which modern "mechanised divisions" have been employed. Yet the narratives show that the bulk of the attacking force was composed of infantry, who were merely carried in lorries and had to dismount before attacking. These would be more precisely described as "motorised" divisions; even so it would appear that most of their vehicles were far from being of a modern kind adequately adapted to movement off the roads. The inability of these temporarily lorry-borne infantry to attack effectively after they had dismounted provided a reminder that mud can be a barrier to men on their feet as well as to men on wheels, especially when the barrier is thickened by machine-guns. In weighing the difficulties also met by the accompanying tanks, account should be taken of the fact that the small Ger-

man and Italian tanks, which have been employed in
Spain, were already recognised as too small, and otherwise unsuited, for surmounting serious obstacles. This
of course does not imply that larger and better machines would be unaffected by mud if it were sufficiently bad. Twenty years ago Passchendaele taught a
lesson in the folly of using tanks in swamp-like conditions, if also of pursuing an offensive by any means in
such conditions. It is as curious a reflection that these
lessons should have been ignored by the Nationalist
leaders as that the natural result should be regarded as
an adverse revelation on mechanisation. Those who
have thoroughly studied the subject of mechanised
warfare have long insisted on the importance of dis-
tinguishing between fully mechanised and merely motorised troops. They have pointed out that, to make
the best of the former and diminish the dangers of air
attack, the scale of man-power and consequently of
superfluous vehicles should be much reduced; that the
force should be composed of armoured vehicles of
high cross-country performance; that it should be
trained to keep off the roads, to move on wide fronts,
and to maintain a state of controlled dispersion. Only
when these conditions are fulfilled is there any reliable
guide to the value of mechanised forces.

Even so, such inferences as can be drawn from
symptoms in Spain tend to support the view, expressed
earlier in this book, that the ultimate general effect of
mechanisation will be towards enhancing the power of
defence, through increasing rapidity of reinforcement

and counter-move, rather than towards reviving the power of the offensive.

The chief threat to the solidity and endurance of modern defence comes from the effect, predominantly moral, of intensive air attack. This has been illustrated in the offensive which the Nationalists, baulked elsewhere, have pursued since the spring against the Basque territory in the north. Constant cloud in the mountains at first hindered the use of the mass of Italian and German aircraft which had been concentrated for the purpose, and so long as this friendly cloak remained to compensate the Basques' lack of air defences they proved able, though only a militia, to hold up the attack of superior ground forces. The experience showed that so long as troops in defence have the spirit to resist, their resistance is likely to prevail even under adverse conditions of training and equipment. A change in the situation came with a temporary improvement of flying conditions, and such progress as the Nationalists subsequently achieved coincided with their opportunities to employ their air superiority as a tactical lever, in loosening the defence of key-positions which offered a well-defined target. Systematic and concentrated air bombardment is hard to endure if there is a lack of direct counter-means, especially where the troops exposed to it know that their resistance on the ground does not suffice to cover their homes, and that their families are suffering a similar bombardment which they can do nothing to check. Air power as exploited against the Basques has revived in a new way the "dual-stretch" of the combatant's instincts which eventually broke down the resistance of the Confederate forces seventy years ago when Sherman made his back-door entry into the South and cut a swathe of devastation through Georgia and the Carolinas.

The development of the War in Spain is symptomatic of the general trend of modern warfare. This serves to blow away sentimental vapourings about the heroic virtues of war, utilised by militaristic nations in generating a warlike spirit among their people. It can no longer be claimed that war is, in common sense, any test of a people's fitness. Or even of their national strength. The most virile and most united people would not be able to withstand another, or even a mere party, inferior to it in all natural qualities if the latter had some decisively superior technical appliance. Fighting spirit itself is a factor of diminishing importance. There is even a prospect that a nation as such may be at the mercy of any gang of moral and physical degenerates which becomes possessed of such an appliance—a reflection which lends irony to the fact that nationalism is being so assiduously cultivated at the very time that science is undermining its foundations. There is, however, another and better prospect, that an apparently weak and unmilitary country where scientific research proceeds under the fairest conditions may come on such a means. That possibility, which is becoming more likely, imparts instability to any warlike calculations, and may thus be a deterrent to any power which is inclined to venture on war on the basis of its own calculable military strength.

In general, the experience of the war in Spain has given cause for more encouragement than discouragement to peaceful peoples. While due allowance must be made for the small scale of the air forces engaged there relatively to that which a general European war would produce, and for the handicap of inadequate ground organisation, it is justifiable to draw two provisional conclusions—first, that air bombing tends to follow the general course of experience with past weapons, and to prove less overwhelming in fulfillment than in anticipation, in practice than in theory; second, that while defence is not yet on equal terms with attack in the air, the deterrent influence of its presence is far more powerful than its actual effect, while the effect attained by the attack decreases disproportionately with the multiplication of defensive means. Pilots as well as peoples are susceptible to psychological stresses.

On land, the experience of the war has strongly supported the evidence of the World War that the defence is paramount at present. This has added significance because relatively small forces in vast areas offered the attack more scope, and a better chance, than it had on the closely packed Western Front. There have been a few successes gained mainly by manoeuvre. But offensives by either side have in general had small effect in proportion to their cost of life. And, even when a local moral breakdown has momentarily cleared the attackers' path, experience has

again confirmed that of the World War in showing
that conditions set a term to their powers of exploiting
it. In taking the offensive each side was embarking on
a venture whose tactical foundations were unsound,
and whose slender chance of any great effect lay in the
psychological sphere—in the possibility that the opponents might be ripe for a moral collapse. Otherwise
a heavy sacrifice of life with little to show was the
probable result. The original circumstances of the campaign, a military revolt against the Government, compelled General Franco to adopt an offensive strategy
if he was to attain his aims; the extent to which his
forces have pursued the offensive tactically would
seem to have been more avoidable, and more dangerous
to his cause. On the other side the contrasting circumstances of a Government without an army helped to
produce a wiser tactical course, and this was long
maintained. Its abandonment by the Government in
February may be traced to later circumstances which
were too strong for restraining calculation. Raw troops
and mass levies are apt to lose morale when kept to
the defensive, though it may be well suited to their
conditions tactically; even trained forces may falter if
thus restrained unless they have been carefully taught
that the highest art of soldiership lies in utilising the
advantages which fire defence and calculated withdrawal offer for entrapping the opponent. None the
less the side which nowadays pins its hopes to attack
courts the risk of undermining its own troops' morale
in the effort. That risk has recently matured first on

the Government side and then on the Nationalists'.

General Franco, who started with the advantage in trained troops, could least afford to waste them: as he has done, not merely under pressure of circumstances. Since the autumn of 1936 he has been increasingly dependent on foreign resources, in far greater measure than his opponents. And as the months have passed it has become clear that his chances of military victory depend on the forces poured in by Italy and Germany —and on these being greatly increased. Otherwise the most probable alternative to stalemate is that continued attacks may turn the scales of war against the attacking side. In that event, the collapse of a cause already undermined may be accelerated by complementary attacks on the part of the side which has conserved its strength better. And then, ironically, from the superficial appearance of victorious advances may once again arise the delusion that the attack has found a way of overcoming the defence.

Contents

PART III—FORECASTS

EUROPE IN ARMS

I

The Defence of Freedom

THE WAR TO EXHAUSTION HAS HAD AS ITS sequel a generation of revolutions in reverse. One by one the nations of the Continent have been engulfed in civil strife, from which they have emerged with a form of government and an attitude to the rights of the individual that is essentially alien to the Anglo-Saxon tradition. England, if now less of an island strategically—because the air has bridged the sea—is more than ever an island politically. That situation calls for serious reflection. Will England stand rocklike amid the totalitarian tide until that tide ebbs? Her constitution for several centuries has had its roots in the growing idea of individual liberty. Her history rests on the reconciliation of that idea with order. In the modern world she has sought, instinctively rather than of plan, to combine the legacy of Greece and Rome. For a time, in the last century, her example had an ever-widening influence; it was embraced, with more enthusiasm than understanding, by nations where the tradition of freedom had no roots. They adopted the form of what they conceived to be her constitution without being infused by its spirit. They tried to pin down to a formula what she, with a practical wisdom born of experience, has never attempted to formulate. The war of 1914–18 interrupted this liberal expansion. Even in England it imposed a check on the process of growth. Abroad, its first effect was, naturally, to strengthen the position of all autocratic governments, and thus stiffen their resistance to reform; ultimately, it produced a cataclysm so disruptive that even those who desired to introduce the rule of right were compelled to maintain their rule by might. Recourse to such means endangered the end, while a just repugnance to them hindered their effectiveness even in preserving the newly established democracies. These conditions were the opportunity of more positive and less scrupulous men, for whom the use of force needed no apology, and a further series of upheavals raised to power a new set of rulers whose revival of authoritarianism was the more intense because authority was fresh to them. Their political gospels might show many different facets, but they had a fundamental similarity of attitude—in their deification of the State as represented by themselves, and their extremely positive negation of the individual's freedom of thought and expression. Alike to Communism and Fascism, uniformity is an ideal, and nonconformity a crime. Moreover, the ideal is expressed by a practice of putting the people into military uniform. This invests with doubt any assertion that a gospel is for home consumption, and makes it inevitably the concern of other peoples.

But for this factor there would be little cause to raise the question of England's power to resist the totalitarian tide. Her tradition of ordered freedom has an older and

a deeper foundation than any regime of compulsory order. It is true that since the war there has been some
erosion of the rights of the individual through the legacy
of war legislation, the intensive growth of social legislation, and the accompanying tendency to bureaucratic
development. But among our people in general the impulses that lead to revolution, and thereby provide opportunity for those who crave autocratic power, seem to
be a diminishing element. Toleration has never been so
widespread, nor violence so widely disfavoured. The decline of the Liberal party, and the consequent loosening
of that sectional label, has helped the spread of liberal
ideas through all parties. And they are strongest of all
among the growing number who find consistent allegiance to a particular party inconsistent with truth: with
that scientific study of conditions which offers the surest
basis of progress. Thus, internally, England's situation
to-day offers a better assurance than at any time since
the war of evolution in accord with her tradition. The
only serious danger to-day lies outside her borders. And
the external danger is also the most probable agent
towards any revival of internal danger. War is a compound menace. It threatens not only the national existence but all that makes existence worth while.

Events abroad have brought this menace to the fore,
and its implications must be faced. At present they are
not being faced squarely. One section looks to the repair
of England's defence arms—and looks no further: the
need of arms is asserted with little regard to whether
they will be effective, and still less to where they may
lead. Another section, forswearing arms, looks so far

ahead that it overlooks the reality of immediate risks:
contemplating a world of common ideals it ignores the
destructive power of force exercised by neighbours who
have different ideals. "Pacifism" and "patriotism" are
hurled from side to side as opposed terms of reproach.
Meantime a large part of the public, confused by the
counter-cries, tends to take the line of least resistance to
the danger. Such passive acceptance of fate does not
even promise the fragile hope that a policy of passive
resistance holds out, while it jeopardizes the building of
actual defences. The dangers of this national division,
and confusion, in the present critical situation ought to
be realized. Without sacrificing the natural diversity
which is the source of vitality it should be possible to
reach some common basis of co-operation among men of
good will. They must combine in building a bridge, unless what each holds dear is to slip into the chasm.

The first need is to achieve a clearer view of differing
points of view. The ardent believer in defence by arms
must try to understand the intellectual position of the
pacifist, instead of hurling denunciations which miss the
mark while marring the atmosphere. The ardent lover of
peace must respond, by giving due weight to the practical case for armed defence. Perhaps the difficulty is
greater for the former, the "instinctive patriots" who are
accustomed to accept unquestioningly so much that
thoughtful men are bound to submit to the test of reason.
They are apt to regard as blasphemy, against the tribal
gods, an attitude that is essentially a searching for truth
and a fervent desire for a true basis of national faith. But

they should be able to see the danger of splitting the nation, and should realize that any persecution of pacifism is the surest way to strengthen it. The problem of reconciling pacifists to the necessity of defence is more complex. The arguments for abjuring force have so clear a moral basis that, in a Christian country, they start with a moral advantage over the arguments for rearmament. In theory, they must command the assent of all decent men, while their simplicity strengthens their appeal. And even on practical grounds there is a stronger case for pure pacifism than is generally realized. The power of non-violent resistance has been demonstrated on occasions, and in spite of its experimental nature it has achieved some notable successes. Its advocates, however, are inclined to overlook the fact that these have been obtained against opponents whose code of morality was fundamentally similar, and whose ruthlessness was thereby restrained. Moreover, its employment against a government, by the spiritually minded members of a religious or political movement, is quite a different matter to its employment in the conflict of nations. To offer any chance of success here, it not only demands a higher collective morale than any army has attained, but requires this fortitude to be shown by a whole people. The effectiveness of an army can be maintained by strong leaders supported by an adequate nucleus of staunch and highly trained troops, since it is the well-aimed shots which mainly count, whereas the effectiveness of non-violent resistance is undermined if a fair proportion of members can be induced, by weakness or self-interest, to serve the opponent's purpose. Comparatively, an army is more dependent on its strongest elements, an unarmed force more dependent on its weakest.

Facing these difficulties honestly, and taking account of prevailing conditions, can any reasonable man hold out the expectation that a nation as a whole could be persuaded to try the tremendous experiment of pure pacifism? If not, its advocacy can only weaken the power of the nation to resist the forces of hostile nations, where pacifism is suppressed. The breakdown of the defences might spell the end of the tradition of freedom as well as of the pacifist aim. The issue cannot be shirked. Those who prize peace for the sake of ideals, not merely peace at any price, have a grave responsibility. If the need of defence be admitted as a practical necessity, it largely lies with them whether the defence is adquate. Their support is essential. By withholding it, they invite the downfall of the home of their ideal. In return for their support, however, they may justly expect guarantees that it shall not be abused; that measures of defence shall not lead to militarization or the curtailment of freedom. Here the Government, the services, and the vocally patriotic have a duty: to avoid offence. Denunciations of pacifism inevitably excite suspicion of the speakers' ultimate aims, and thus stiffen opposition. Propaganda for defence too often fails to convey any idea beyond arming because others are doing it. None but the unthinking and those whose patriotism is mere self-interest would regard defence as worth while if, in the process of defence, the spirit of the country were to be extinguished and only the husk remain.

But something more than a working agreement on actual measures is needed. This is too passive—and passive defence will not suffice against a vigorous challenge. There is overflowing vigour in the foreign nationalisms, even though it be obtained by a contraction of spirit which tends to ultimate exhaustion. Men who are infused with a faith, even a false one, will beat men who have no faith; only a good one can withstand the impact. Those who complain of the younger generation's lack of patriotism should, rather, reproach themselves for their failure to define and teach patriotism in higher terms than the mere preservation of a geographical area, its inhabitants and their material interests. Such a material appeal offers no adequate inspiration, nor cause for sacrifice, to the young. Those who are concerned with practical questions of defence ought to realize the practical importance of ideals, especially in arousing the British people. Again and again it has been found that the economic appeal had little power to overcome their characteristic inertia until something stirred their latent idealism. The man who does not take due account of this element is a fool. Its prevalence, as well as its purity, would seem to have increased in recent times. The significance of repeated demonstrations of its power is the greater because it has had no prophet to express it adequately. The professed patriots have concentrated on a doctrine of national self-preservation, and their appeals have had a metallic ring. This marks a relapse. Two generations back, Kipling provided the British people with a gospel of Empire which raised Imperialism above mere materialism: to-day its crudity jars, but it has found no replacement. There is need for a new vision—one bigger than Kipling's, and better. To gain this we must grasp the elements that matter in the Anglo-Saxon tradition— above all, the spirit of freedom. In freedom, truth is perceived and justice promised. From the trinity, vitality springs. If Fascism and Communism can raise enthusiasm among the young, how much better sources have we from which to generate it. At the same time it requires, not a diminished but an intensified self-criticism. For in such self-criticism is the foundation of a faith that can alone assure secure progress. The interests of the State should never demand injustice to the individual, nor any restriction of freedom save where it is used for active interference with others' freedom—justice and freedom are the true interests of the State. Fear and suspicion poison the well-springs of a people—their absence from the atmosphere is the test of whether the State is fitted to fulfil its end. Once aware of the essential elements of the tradition, we betray it if we commit or condone a breach of them within our own land. In upholding them against external threats we have a cause worth defence, and sacrifice. It offers a common rallying ground for all parties, and classes. For here patriotism and pacifism are combined in a positive form—and faith.

PART I: FORCES

2

The Air Forces of Europe

THE ATMOSPHERE OF EUROPE IS BECOMING heavily charged. Its tendencies inevitably have a reminder of 1914, yet with differences. People everywhere are talking of "war". It is easier for men to see the ways in which war may come than how it can be avoided. The hopes that they express have no firm ring of confidence. On the other hand, there is curiously little accent of fear in the forebodings they express. Fear may be the ultimate source of the forces that are gathering, but it does not emerge on the surface. France has been fearing things so long, and so many things, that the edge of her fears may have become dulled. This may help to explain the strange state of resignation that seems to have overtaken the French just at the time when the dangers they have long anticipated are coming closer to realization. Elsewhere on the Continent it is difficult to gauge the measure of the fear because it is submerged in the intoxication that is so palpable. Men are once again talking and singing, with a martial fervour that sends a chill through a sober listener. It is true that they will make intermittent declarations of their repugnance to the idea of another war—

if this be true, they have a peculiar way of expressing
their dislike. But different as the angles from which the
peoples of Europe are viewing the possibility of war,
there is a common slant in the view they take of its
nature.

Their thoughts instinctively fly upwards—and their
imagination flies faster. Memory, of air attacks in the last
war, is as much the propellant as any knowledge of air
developments since. To anyone who analyzes the comparatively slight material results of air raids in 1914–18,
it is remarkable to find what a profound psychological
impression they made, and have left. Small as was the
force employed in these raids, it caused a greater and
wider nerve strain than any other agent of warfare. The
effects have not disappeared with the cessation of the
cause: they are traceable in the general tendency among
the public, whenever they think of war, for the thought
to be associated immediately with the idea of being
bombed from the air. And from this apprehension
springs a natural exaggeration.

During these last years, the armaments race has begun
again. It is an ominous reality. But here again imagination travels faster than the facts. In 1934 the British public was startled by the declaration of a great newspaper
magnate that Germany had 25,000 military aircraft. In
1935 he informed the House of Lords that Germany
possessed 10,000 bombers each capable of carrying about
a ton of explosives. If the estimate had not mounted as
one might have expected, considering that there had been
a year's interval for expansion, the picture was certainly
painted on a large canvas. The Russians have a reputa-

tion for generous-size estimates of any German military preparations: at the same period the Assistant Commissar for War credited the Germans with a total of 3700 military aircraft, including reserves. Even this figure was considerably in excess of what French experts calculated—and the French, since 1914, are not inclined to minimize any menace that Germany possesses.

If fear be the predisposing cause of war, ignorance is the most potent of the factors that nourish it. The fear of the unknown breaks down armies in wartime; in peace time it drives nations, like the Gadarene swine, down to the abyss. Unhappily, it is again becoming epidemic today through a fresh wave of "secrecy". Fear and secrecy react on each other. "Spy-mania" is one of the products. This ugly rash is again breaking out on the face of Europe; and no symptom could be more ominous. Its justification is probably slender, as usual. For the knowledge that matters is rarely gained by the methods that thrill the lover of sensational spy-stories: safer, in every sense, is the knowledge that comes by the application of ordinary deductive methods to a mass of data that are common property, fitting together the insignificant fragments on a foundation of technical understanding until they form a mosaic from which a clear picture emerges.

Air strength is normally reckoned in terms of first line aircraft—which represents the number of machines actually in service with formed units. Subject to certain qualifications that I shall touch upon, it gives a reasonable idea of the number of aircraft which could be engaged on the outbreak of war, and thereby enables one

to arrive at some calculation of the scale of air attack
that a country might launch.

The creation and expansion of the German Air Force
has been carried out in such a haze of secrecy as to foster
exaggerated assumptions. Yet there is reason to doubt
whether its first line strength exceeded 1200 machines at
the end of 1936. Expansion, however, has been moving
rapidly, with vigorous governmental aid at every step, to
overcome the disadvantages of a late start. By the spring of
1937 it is expected that the German Air Force will have
attained what is believed to be its immediate goal—a first
line strength of 1500 machines. That it did not reach this
earlier was due to the difficulty of training personnel and
organizing units as fast as the manufacture of machines,
which has been proceeding at a rate that was probably
in excess of the capacity to absorb them. The accident
rate in training is reported to have been extremely high,
although the details have been hidden. Another significant feature of the German Air Force is the high
proportion of bombers of various types. Fully half the
force appears to be composed of bomber squadrons of
various kinds, and more than half of these are equipped
with large machines that can carry a bomb-load of upwards of a ton, with a radius (out and back distance) of
about four hundred miles—far enough to reach the capitals of any of Germany's neighbours. This may help to
account for the reluctance which the German leaders
have recently shown to consider any agreed check upon
air bombing.

Germany, also, has specialized in the construction of
civil aircraft that were easily and quickly convertible

into effective military machines, and probably a further 200 could have been reckoned on this account. This asset, however, is now losing much of its old significance with the achievement of the air force expansion. So long as Germany was trying to hide the fact that she was developing a military air force it was convenient to have a reserve of pseudo-civil machines that could be converted into bombers in emergency. Now the need for this device has passed. Nevertheless the pilots and personnel carry out several months' regular training each year, and there is little doubt that in war they would be immediately formed into regular squadrons, equipped with military aircraft which are held ready for them in peace. The civil aircraft themselves would more likely be utilized for training purposes. There are also the auxiliary and sports associations, in which well over five thousand pilots are said to be in training; from these might emerge enough squadrons to form an additional force of 300-400 machines, besides providing reserve pilots for the Regular Air Force.

The strength of the British Air Force, before an expansion programme was somewhat hurriedly embarked upon in face of the ominous European situation, amounted to only 880 first line machines. The process of expansion, moreover, has been complicated by Italy's invasion of Abyssinia and the consequent tension in the Mediterranean: the diversion of instructors to emergency duty naturally interfered with the training of new personnel. At the end of 1936 the total regular strength was just over 1100. But the needs of India and the other overseas territories, as well as of the Navy, reduced the total

regular strength at home to a little under 900 first line
machines. Under the present programme of expansion,
whose completion has suffered from delays, it should
reach a total of 1500 by the spring or summer of 1937,
and 1750 by the autumn.

France long had the highest strength among the Western Powers, her total first line strength, being at one time
not far short of 1700 machines; it is now probably about
1500. But of these barely 1100 are available at home, the
rest being overseas, in North Africa, the Levant, Indo-
China, etc. Moreover, most of the French machines are
not of a very modern type, although new types of
greatly improved performance are expected to come into
service gradually from the early months of this year.
The number, too, is being increased fifty per cent. An
existing factor which has to be taken into account is that
France's proportion of bombers is much less than Germany's. But the new French machines will be of much
larger bomb-capacity than at present.

The Russian Air Force is now the greatest in Europe.
Its first line strength is reported to be over 3500 machines, and may be as high as 4000. It includes at least
500 large bombers of long radius—of which, because of
her geographical distances, she has made a special point.
The strength of the Russian Air Force, together with its
striking range, forms the ground on which Hitler is
claiming to go beyond the level of parity with the air
forces of his Western neighbours. Another feature which
Russia has developed is the employment of swarms of
machines designed for the attack upon ground targets,
in conjunction with the army. Many of her machines are

of an obsolescent type, but she is reported to have made better progress than many people would have expected in the creation of the ground organization necessary for the efficient use of such a large air force.

Italy is another country where the veil of secrecy has been tightly drawn. Since the expansion which followed the coming of the Abyssinian War, her actual first line strength is probably about 1500 machines. Out of this nearly 200 are said to be still in Eritrea and Somalia, engaged in clearing up the Abyssinian situation, and about the same number is in Libya and the Dodecanese. But Italy can probably exercise the strategic mobility of her air force better than any other country with overseas possessions. For she can concentrate at home in peace, for training, and yet reinforce Libya and the Dodecanese at short notice whenever required. This strategic mobility is growing with the extending range of aircraft—and Abyssinia as well will soon be reinforcible by air as easily as Libya is to-day. Italy has now a large output of new types of bombers of high performance, with a speed of about 220 m.p.h. and a radius of nearly five hundred miles. These have been turned out by the factories as fast as possible. With such a radius, it would be possible, from Libya, to reach not only Alexandria but Port Said, and also the ports in Southern Greece. Only the extreme ends of the Mediterranean would be beyond their stretch.

Such risks as these have called for reflection by the statesmen whose countries carry the main burden of the League and would have to bear the brunt of any "mad-dog" attack. It is common knowledge that when the possibility arose in the autumn of 1935, the bulk of the Brit-

ish fleet was withdrawn from its historic base of Malta to
the extremities of the Mediterranean—a precaution that
was a striking testimony to the strategic influence of air-
power on sea-power, and the more striking in view of
the way that sailors tended to depreciate the new weapon
so long as hard facts had not to be faced. That candid
recognition of the risk may prove of practical benefit in
promoting the adaptation of their own defence systems
to modern conditions. Moreover, it gives no encouragement to Italy, on a sane calculation, to precipitate the
risk. For her strategic situation as a whole has weaknesses
so marked that, on a long view, they should be a check
on rash impulses. Apart from the fact that so large a part
of her land forces and resources are engulfed in East
Africa, precariously dependent on a tenuous lifeline
from the homeland, Italy's own situation has handicaps
that are inherent in geography: her long coastline, the
narrowness of the country, and the nearness of her main
centres to the sea or to neighbouring frontiers, are factors that cannot be ignored. The factories which produce her new long-range instruments of warfare are
themselves within uncomfortably short range of the less
obvious points from which the forces of other countries
might take off. Compared with France, for example, the
strategic situation of Italy is on balance unfavourable for
any contest in the air. Her vital centres are far more ac-
cessible than are those of France to the Italian air bases.
The comparison may be extended from the question of
the moment to the European problem as a whole. The
more one reflects on the involved problems of modern
warfare, the more importance seems to attach to the

factor of "vulnerability"—the relative vulnerability of the different countries—in any comparison of strengths.

This in turn has a bearing upon the research for technical surprise which is now being so actively pursued. Those who contemplate taking the offensive in any future European war are impelled to seek a new master-key both by the certainties and uncertainties of the problem. They are forced to recognize that the methods of the last war will not suffice; that nothing but a protracted struggle and an inconclusive result can be expected from the use of armies equipped with the weapons of 1918 merely improved. They fear that such a prolongation of the issue may produce developments that cannot be foreseen, causing a rapid shifting of the balance. The combination of these thoughts is an urge to the search for quick results. In 1914, the military chiefs hoped to decide the issue within a few weeks, and bent their efforts towards this object. That was short enough—and much shorter than the event, after their plans had miscarried. Now, they are coming to the view that the first few days, or even hours, may be crucial, and to see that unless they can obtain a decisive advantage within this brief time it may be unattainable on any calculable basis. Hence their eagerness to find new weapons that may overcome defence without past delays.

The scope for such technical surprise is not limited to the invention of new weapons. It may be obtained by an unexpected multiplication of strength. In 1914 the Germans surprised the French by incorporating their reserve formations in their striking force, thus deploying nearly double the numbers that the French expected to meet in the opening clash. This device may be repeated to-day with air forces, and it is the possibility which lends instability to the system of calculating air strength in terms of first line machines. For each first line machine, most countries aim to maintain three or four in reserve, to make up the wastage that is likely to occur during the first few months of a struggle, before the factories can attain their expanded war rate of production. But an aggressive-minded power may consider that the risk of being caught short at the end of a month or two is less than that of failing to gain the maximum advantage in the first days. Or at any rate that the prospects of early success are worth the risk. Hence, it may decide to employ a part of its reserve aircraft with its first line units, increasing their size or their number. The extent to which it can do this, and the extent of the surprise attained, will depend on the efficiency of its arrangements.

But if the gamble fails the last state may be worse than the first. There are so many incalculables. A quantitative advantage on one side may offset some unrealized qualitative advantage on the other; either may be upset by some inadequately appreciated advantage in vulnerability, or by the belated discovery that the effect of an attack is not equal to what was necessary to repay the effort and justify the risk. Weather conditions, psychological conditions, economic conditions, political contingencies all play their part in complicating the problem. The uncertainty which exists as to the actual state of the various nations' forces is nothing to the uncertainty which prevails as to their effect. If the former engenders the fear which leads to war, the latter justifies fears that may deter the decision to embark upon war. It is a certainty that the vitals of each country are exposed to its neighbours' action. There is one greater certainty—that there is more uncertainty than ever before about all the other factors with which strategists and statesmen must reckon. Compared with the present state of flux, it was simple to make military calculations in the past. The elements of strength were to a great extent calculable. To embark on war then was no greater hazard than that of betting on the favourite—and yet the favourite has often lost. To-day, it is like backing a horse that has never run, and whose breeding even is unknown. Any professional gambler might think it wise to refrain; statesmen should be as wise.

3

The Armies of Europe—
The Totalitarian Powers

NAPOLEON DELIVERED HIMSELF OF THE SAY-
ing that "Providence marches with the big battalions".
He was often careless about self-contradiction and also
about the way his sayings might be misinterpreted. This
one was not altogether borne out in his practice, although he certainly relied on weight of numbers more
than most of the great Captains. Such a tendency was
inevitable owing to his disregard of the possibilities of
making his forces qualitatively decisive through superior
training or superior weapons. It was fostered by his unlimited resources—until the man-power of France was
exhausted. Even so, his victories were obtained more by
manœuvring power in massing superior numbers at the
decisive point than by a mere total superiority.

His words, however, made a deep impression. And
they were read in the more obvious sense. A generation
later his famous German interpreter, Clausewitz, expressed the conviction that "superiority in numbers becomes every day more decisive". He at any rate had

more excuse than the military authorities who, in all countries, have repeated his creed for a century. For when he wrote, the mechanical age was only dawning, whereas his followers persisted in this delusion while mechanical weapons were continually multiplying in nature and effect. They forgot how Alexander conquered Asia, how Hannibal defeated the Roman armies in their own land, how Belisarius reconquered the Roman Empire, how·Genghis Khan swept over Asia and Europe, with forces far smaller than those opposing them. They forgot the still clearer proof of the value of superior armaments which was provided when Strongbow conquered Ireland with a few hundred knights, an astonishing lesson in the power of a technically decisive handful which was repeated in Cortés's conquest of Mexico, Pizarro's conquest of Peru, and Clive's conquests in India.

When the World War came in 1914, the fallacy of the "big battalions" was exposed by the mechanical progress which enabled one man sitting behind a machine-gun to account for more than a score, or sometimes a hundred, or sometimes even a thousand, who were advancing upon him with rifle and bayonet. The more the number of the attackers, the more the number of the dead—that was all in many cases. The contrast between qualitative and quantitative values was exemplified in another way at Cambrai on November 20th, 1917, where the use of only 378 tanks and some 4000 tankmen to assist a mere six divisions of infantry, produced a greater gain of ground and a greater shock to the enemy at a cost of some 5000 casualties, than the use of several dozen divisions had achieved at Ypres in a three months' effort at a cost of 400,000 casualties. The contrast also illuminated the qualitative difference between different technical means—for at Ypres the British Higher Command rested their hopes of breaking down the enemy's resistance on the use of 3000 guns and 120,000 gunners, who fired some four and a half million shells in the preliminary bombardment alone.

Yet, in spite of all the experience which shows that numbers have little real meaning, the governments and generals of Europe still, as a whole, continue to count their forces in terms of "numerical men". And the public is naturally of the same tendency. Such figures are easier to grasp than the difficult and intricate assessment of qualitative values. If they throw little light on the military problem they at least help to show the taxpayers' burden—the pay and upkeep of the individual soldier— forms by far the biggest proportion of any military budget. Since no survey of the armies of Europe would seem factual without these "false" figures, I will insert a few in this account. They are as accurate as can be determined under the conditions of censorship and mystification which now prevail in many parts of Europe. And if the sum should be a million or so out, it will not much matter militarily from any practical point of view. The real power of the armies of the three great totalitarian states, with which this chapter is concerned in particular, does not lie in their numbers of men under arms. The vast numbers, however, have significance as the symptoms of an impediment compulsorily contracted by the nature of such states.

GERMANY

Since the advent of the Nazi regime, the German Army has carried out a great expansion and undergone a great transformation, not altogether to its qualitative advantage. By the terms of the Treaty of Versailles it was limited to a strength of 100,000 men voluntarily enlisted on a long-service basis, and was forbidden the use of tanks, aircraft, and heavy artillery. These compulsory limitations encouraged an attempt to surpass them subtly by developing a force of superior quality and mobility. Surprise became its keynote—"every action", declared the post-war German manuals, "should be based on surprise . . . ruses and wiles of every kind ought always to be used to deceive the enemy". General von Seeckt, the rebuilder of the German Army after the war, had been the brain of Field-Marshal von Mackensen in the war, devising the plans which led to the Gorlice breakthrough against the Russians in 1915, and to later successes. He gave the post-war army a doctrine of mobility, and put forward the view that a small, quick-moving, quick-hitting army of picked troops could, under modern conditions, discount the numerical superiority of an old-fashioned mass army. That view was genuinely shared by some of the more original-minded German officers. But the majority merely made a virtue of necessity; brought up in the creed of mass, they hankered after the size which to them still represented strength and, no less important, a reflected prestige. Similarly, despite the experience of the war and their straitened post-war means, they still clung to the old belief in the offensive; officers like the present Field-Marshal von Blomberg, who sought to adapt tactics to modern conditions and advocated such methods as the luring defensive, found it difficult to convince the bulk of their comrades.

The idea of the "qualitative" professional army had not really taken firm root when the Hitler revolution gave the Army a chance to revert to the old love of mass. The Nazi movement of its very nature made such a reversion almost inevitable. Many of the Regular officers were undoubtedly apprehensive of the effect of diluting their carefully trained units with undisciplined enthusiasts of the Brown Shirt type, and found still more cause for concern in the claim of the Brown Shirt leaders for a share in the officering of the new national army. They were ready to welcome all the support that the new regime gave to the growth of the Army and of martial ideas, but not to accept a partnership in the control. Their policy prevailed, on this point, helped by Hitler's need of the Army to maintain what he had created, or unloosed.

At Geneva, before she left the League, Germany had claimed the right to expand her army of 100,000 men, organized in seven divisions, to an army of 300,000. While the statesmen argued, the process of expansion went on. The aim was to create a force of twenty-one divisions. The manufacture of tanks, artillery, machine-guns, and aircraft was rapidly developed. The way for conscription was paved by the introduction of six months' labour service, and the training was so directed that the Labour Corps soon came to have a marked military value—more, indeed, than the Brown Shirts.

Then, in March, 1935, conscription for the Army was announced, and, simultaneously, the expansion of the Army to thirty-six divisions, organized in twelve army corps. The news came as a shock in neighbouring countries, increased by the importance customarily accorded to numbers. Yet, curiously, there was a tendency to underestimate the new total through ignoring the proportion of corps and army troops; 450,000 was suggested as the probable figure, whereas it was likely to exceed 550,000. The first contingent of conscripts of the 1914 class (now aged 21) was called up in October. An average year was expected to yield about 300,000 young men. At the same time the men between twenty-one and thirty-five (the classes 1900–13) who represent Germany's lost classes of trained reserves have been called up for short periods of training lasting six weeks to two months.

In August, 1936, a fresh step was taken, by extending the period of conscript service from one year to two. This may be partly designed to offset the lean birth-rate years represented by the 1915 to 1919 classes, but is likely to increase the total under arms. Moreover, it is known that Germany has formed three armoured divisions which are additional to the thirty-six divisions provided for by the Army Law of March 16th, 1935, while there are reports of the formation of two more. The fact has a reflection on Hitler's declaration in the Reichstag a few days later: "The German Government have announced the extent of the expansion of the new German

defence forces. In no circumstances will they depart
therefrom." It would seem that a further increase is not
regarded as a departure.

These new-style formations were not shown to the
foreign officers and military publicists who were invited
to see the German Army at work in the autumn manœuvres of 1935 and 1936. In the infantry divisions
which have been seen, the transport of the battalions and
the field artillery was still horse-drawn, but they were
well provided with machine-guns, anti-tank guns, and
mortars. The division has some 400 machine-guns, light
and heavy, and their proportion of anti-tank guns—two
and a half pounders drawn by a light car—is higher than
in the French or any other army; they form a divisional
unit of three companies with a total of about forty-two
guns. The most interesting new feature of the division is
a mechanized reconnaissance group, which comprises a
company of armoured cars or light tanks, one of anti-
tank guns, one of four light mortars, one of machine-
guns, and two companies of infantry in lorries. They are
used to push ahead of the division's advance, seize tactical points, and occupy them with machine-guns, and
then press on to a fresh objective. The staple of the division is composed of three infantry regiments, each of
which is formed of three battalions, a mortar company, a
machine-gun company, and a troop of cavalry. The battalion is organized in three "rifle" companies, each having nine light machine-guns.

There is an apparent shortage of officers, owing partly
to the wise desire to maintain the standard, if also to a
reluctance to give commissions except to those who have

passed through the orthodox professional channels. But the training of the troops has made a strong impression on those who have watched it; they move more dispersed than the French, and are no less active in movement, while their equipment is far more modern—the Versailles Treaty has here had its compensations. Their new 105 mm. field-howitzers and their anti-aircraft guns are highly efficient weapons. But the general composition of these divisions and their handling show little advance on the ideas of the last war. With increase of size the German Army seems to have rather lost sight of the need for subtlety and surprise which Seeckt insisted on in the post-war era.

There is more prospect in the new armoured divisions. They are said to consist of three parts, one for probing, one for hitting, and one for holding. The "punch" is formed by a tank brigade, which is believed to consist of three regiments totalling about 600 tanks. The number of mechanized vehicles in the division as a whole is said to be nearly two thousand. At present the tanks are of a fast but light kind, weighing only about six tons, with two machine-guns in a turret capable of all-round fire. The Germans are seeking a larger, "medium" tank, but it is doubtful if a satisfactory one has yet been produced. Against a country with an open frontier or an army inadequately equipped with anti-tank guns, their new armoured divisions might prove a formidable factor in the opening phase of a war, but there is cause for doubt whether the German Army has yet developed either the equipment or the tactics to solve the problems created by a strong and thoroughly modern defence.

RUSSIA

The Red Army, by contrast, is undoubtedly the most powerful in its tank forces, while also the most original in methods, although new and old ideas are strangely intermingled. The most archaic feature is the prominent role given to horsed cavalry—no less than sixteen cavalry divisions are maintained—and the way they are handled. On manœuvres great masses of horsemen are plunged into tank-infested areas with little regard to the differing degrees of vulnerability. In peace it looks like a colossal circus; in war it would probably mean a huge cemetery. This Russian attempt to repeat Balaclava in face of machine-guns is evidence that the Red Army has not succeeded so far as its progress in other directions suggests in shedding the mental conventions of its predecessor.

The reliance on mass is a general symptom. In numbers of men the Red Army far exceeds any other. A population which has now grown to 170,000,000 provides an annual contingent of recruits which in recent years has always been well over a million and this year is over two million. The peace-time strength of the army has now been raised to 1,300,000. They provide eighty-four infantry divisions apart from other formations. The men taken for the Regular Army do two years continuous service, while those who are not required for this do several months' training in the territorial militia. The Regular Army now represents 73 per cent of the total forces, and the Territorial Militia 27 per cent. It is said that the Red Army chiefs could mobilize 6,000,000 men at a fortnight's notice, and that by 1938 the total trained reserves will reach 10,000,000. This apparently does not include the youths below military age who, to the number of several millions, are receiving preliminary training under the auspices of the Osoaviatkhim and the Young Communist League. More significant is the statement that upwards of half a million have qualified as skilled parachute-jumpers and many thousands as aeroplane or glider pilots.

The bulk of the Army is maintained in the West, but the Far Eastern Army is said to number nearly 300,000 men, while the doubling of the track of the Trans-Siberian railway facilitates its reinforcement in emergency. But as Tukhachevski pointed out in his 1935 report: "If the Germans had to expend some fifteen million kilometre-tons in order to concentrate one infantry division in Liége by means of the railway from Berlin, 200 million kilometre-tons are required of us in order to transfer such a division from Moscow to Vladivostok. Thus we must be very cautious in counting on the rapid transfer of considerable masses of troops over so-called internal operation lines." The strain on the railway for supply has been much reduced by accumulating supplies on the spot in order to make the Far Eastern Army self-sufficient—it has been wittily said that to the soldiers stationed here the tin-opener is almost as indispensable as the rifle. At the same time agriculture and munition factories are being developed here as a more permanent foundation for military effort. This is part of the general scheme by which the industries of Russia are being organized and distributed on a strategic basis—with a predominant easterly trend in order to safeguard them from hostile air attack. The largest source of munitions is now established in the almost inaccessible area near the Ural Mountains. But this only solves half the problem. If the Red Army attempts to concentrate its immense forces to act in any particular theatre there will be an inevitable congestion of the routes of supply in that area. Here lies a continual danger of breakdown.

The units of this mass are certainly far more impressive in quality than the old Czarist Army. The discipline is unmistakably good, yet free from the old brutality. The men's bearing on the march combines smartness with elasticity. In physique and intelligence they look a very good type. The officers are professionally enthusiastic and much better educated than their predecessors —no army takes a keener interest in foreign ideas and all news of military progress. On manœuvres there is much evidence of skilled organization and staffwork. The elimination of the corruption which was rampant on the administrative side of the Czarist Army should alone go far to reduce the risks of defeat through shortage of equipment and supplies.

The most striking features of the Army are its development of tank and air-borne units. There are said to be about 6000 tanks—over a thousand have been seen on manœuvres in one area alone. The small number of breakdowns is evidence of their mechanical efficiency as well as of the standard of training in the crews. If the designs show no marked originality, and are obviously indebted to various foreign models, it would seem that the

Russians have had the ability to adopt and adapt the best points of each. There are great numbers of two-men light tanks which can "swim" rivers and are based on the Carden-Loyd amphibian, first produced in Britain by the Vickers firm. They have also quantities of rather larger machines copied from the 6-ton Vickers. But the machine on which they mainly rely for the modern-style cavalry role is one developed from the American Christie tank. It is well-armoured, weighs about twelve tons, and yet has a speed of over 30 m.p.h. on its tracks, while for long strategic moves these can be taken off and the tank then runs on its bogie wheels. Beyond this, to deliver the decisive assault there is a "medium" tank of no less than twenty-seven tons, carrying a gun of field-artillery calibre as well as machine-guns, yet travelling almost as fast as the Christie-type tank. They have even a small number of "Heavy" tanks, which look like moving fortresses and must weigh at least fifty tons. But, in face of the growing power and variety of anti-tank defence, the Russians prefer to rely on machines of high speed and good obstacle-crossing capacity combined with a fair thickness of armour, rather than increase weight and size at the expense of pace.

While they are now ahead of all other countries in the development of armoured mobile forces, their ideas on the use of such forces are not so well thought out; here they seem to have assimilated many ideas from abroad without digesting them. That, at any rate, is the impression gained from a study of their published views and from personal discussions. Likewise on their manœuvres the higher tactical handling of these forces is not equal to the actual handling of the machines by their crews. This reflection applies also to the handling of the ordinary infantry forces, and their formations are apt to offer too good a target. The undue disregard of the effects of modern fire is even to be noticed in the methods employed in their low-flying attacks on ground columns which are much favoured; these seemed to invite casualties needlessly. This general tendency may be in accord with the Russian tradition, but the scales of warfare are tilting increasingly against it. If it is inherent in a doctrine of war which contemplates the use of masses, that is no reason for believing that the masses, despite their increased efficiency, will prove capable of overcoming modern defence. The Russians might have a better prospect if they relied simply on their mechanized forces. For this would also minimize the worst risk they run in taking an offensive with such vast numbers—that the military machine will break down under the burden on its own communications when the strain is increased by the pressure of air attack.

In one way the Russians, however, are better equipped than any army to produce the enemy's breakdown, and even earlier. The agent lies in their new parachute forces, which were much in evidence during this autumn's manœuvres. In one area, for example, a force of 1200 men together with 150 machine-guns and 18 light field-guns was carried 100 miles in troop-carrying aircraft and dropped on an aerodrome behind the enemy's front. Within eight minutes of the release of the parachutes the force had assembled on the ground and driven off the defenders. The spectacular nature of such an operation may be as likely to make professional soldiers sceptical of its potentialities as to cause an exaggerated estimate of its menace among the public.

It is easy to perceive the practical difficulties which such an expedition might encounter if carried out under war conditions; the dangers it might run both in its passage through the air, in the descent to the ground, and in maintaining itself when landed. Nevertheless, any instrument of surprise starts with a big advantage in war—audacity pays, especially when allied with mobility. Because of its range and power of variability the "parachute stroke" has possibilities that it would be foolish to underrate. Its indirect strategic influence may be much greater than its actual results.

All armies, and nearly all commanders, are acutely susceptible to the threat of a blow in the back, and to the interruption of their communications. The knowledge that the enemy has parachute forces that can be dropped near important bridges or other crucial points in their rear is likely to increase this fear. The risk may well cause the higher command to strengthen all detachments and posts on the lines of communication, thus producing a subtraction of force from the main concentration many times larger than the parachute forces which the enemy possesses. Added to this is the psychological strain. Thus, by the mere threat of their existence such forces have a promise of great effect—greater than any damage they may actually do.

ITALY

In view of the essential antithesis between mass and mobility it is a curious phenomenon that both are being simultaneously developed all over the Continent, without regard to the consequences. No country carries quite so far as Italy the conception of the "nation in arms". The male child is put in uniform when he is scarcely out of the cradle and may stay in it until he is put in the grave—since the hard-worked Italian peasant is often not very long-lived, even apart from the risks of war. At six years of age he is enrolled in the "Balilla del Lupa" (Wolf Cubs), in which besides wearing uniform he is taught to march, to shoot with the rifle and the machine-gun, to wear gas-masks and carry out anti-gas drill, and to inure himself to life under canvas. Boys who are bad at drill are treated as if they had failed to pass their scholastic examinations for promotion to a higher form. At eight he enters the ordinary Balilla corps, and continues there until eighteen, when he undergoes a more intensive system of military training, until at twenty-one he is called up for his conscript service with the Army, which normally lasts eighteen months. After his release he has to carry on his post-military training until the age of fifty-five—and even then he joins the civilian cohorts that are part of the civil mobilization scheme during war-time. The Italian Press was unusually accurate when it applauded this introduction of life-service with the remark that history had no parallel for such nation-wide militarization.

The actual number of the Italian Army is a variable

quantity. In the past it has usually been about 400,000 men, but shortly before the Abyssinian War it was raised to 600,000, and during this 1,000,000 were mobilized. In addition the Fascist Militia totals some 400,000 men. The Army, exclusive of the colonies, is organized in thirteen Army Corps, yielding a total of thirty-one infantry divisions. There are also three mobile divisions mainly of motorized troops, with a small proportion of armoured vehicles. Tanks have not been much developed. They have a few hundred Fiat tanks, but these are very small and limited in obstacle-crossing capacity. They are mainly used as armoured machine-guns to assist the infantry attack.

The infantry division comprises nine battalions, as is usual on the Continent, but until recently three of these were merely kept in skeleton. It is rather weaker in artillery support and also in automatic fire-power than the French. The Italian Army's progress towards mechanization was for long retarded by lack of money, reluctance to be dependent on outside fuel supplies, and the fact that its probable theatres of war were mountainous, thus seeming to offer small scope for mechanized mobility. On the other hand, this type of country has had an influence on the training of the infantry, which has aimed to develop agility by a most strenuous course of physical exercise. The hillsides near any military centre are dotted with gymnastic apparatus, and it is astonishing to see whole companies of men going through a series of vaulting, jumping and balancing exercises which seem severe enough to test a professional acrobat. Likewise the marching of the Italian infantry, both in pace and distance, seems all the more remarkable when one takes note of the slender scale of rations on which these physical feats are performed. They have also begun to exploit a new kind of mobility by following the Russian lead in forming parachute units. In mountain warfare these may have notable effect, as a pass or narrow valley can be held by a few men against many, so that by dropping these parachute units to seize such points in the enemy's rear his reinforcement may be prevented, his supplies interrupted, or his retreat cut off.

By a curious contrast, the higher training of the Italian Army had until recently a tendency to restrain rather than exploit the use of its natural assets. Tactical methods were even more deliberate than in the French Army. In part, this was inspired by the aim of correcting the haphazard ways of the past by a rigorous mental discipline attuned to the new national trend. If it served a practical purpose, it certainly had the less beneficial effect of cramping manœuvre and tactical mobility. Operation orders were so long and detailed that, after reckoning the time for writing and reading them, they seemed to leave little time for executing them—if the enemy were not to be allowed too much grace.

It was thus, in form and in outlook, an old-style army which was shipped out from Italy to Eritrea in 1935. Mechanized vehicles and aircraft were no more than a trimming to the masses of infantry. Yet the trimmings, coupled with the primitive enemy's similar obsession with mass, saved the Italians from the impasse, and even peril, to which their own old-fashioned ideas had brought them. In the outcome, the campaign was determined by

the progressive success of the machine in overcoming
human and natural obstacles. As the data of the campaign
have become available, analysis has tended to confirm
the contemporary inference that the machine-gun and
the gas-projector proved the decisive weapons, aircraft
the decisive arm, and mechanization in general the
foundation of the Italians' success. It forms a striking
vindication of those who, in the face of doubts and obstruction, have for years foreshadowed the importance
of these new factors. For Europe this war is a writing on
the wall—and the more significant because it has been engraved on a remote mountain-wall. For here was a theatre
of war so wild and rugged, and so strategically inaccessible, that aircraft and landcraft were operating under
an exceptional handicap.

The handicap on their action was at first increased by
a handicap on their effect which sprang from the methods of the Italian command. They began the invasion of
Abyssinia after the style of the invading hosts in 1914.
By relying on mass they impeded their own mobility, so
that what was gained by the advent of mechanized means
of movement was largely offset by using them merely to
feed and maintain great masses of infantry. The supply
of such large forces as were employed demanded a well-
developed system of roads. The building of these roads
called for a great number of labourers, together with the
troops to protect them. To feed and otherwise maintain
them caused a great increase in the transport demands
and in the traffic over the new-built roads. That scale of
traffic destroyed the roads almost as fast as they were

built. So the difficulties were multiplied by the very means taken to overcome them.

Thus the Abyssinian War began by providing a fresh illustration, in a somewhat different form, of the lesson of the last European war—that armies are impeded more than helped by their own growth, so that quantitative superiority of force carries its own antidote. That experience merely confirmed the neglected warning of the famous eighteenth century master of war, Marshal Saxe, that "multitudes serve only to perplex and embarrass". He saw, like Sherman a century later, that there is a limit, determined by mobility, to what one may call the *economic size* of an army. It takes unusual art to gauge —mass and mobility are hard to reconcile. Unless the mean, or means, can be found, the use of force is liable to be stultified by its own forces.

It was fortunate for the Italians that there was no air force to oppose them. That missing factor was their salvation from something worse than congestion and internal disorder. At the end of 1935, after three months' campaign, the Italian masses were at a standstill with nothing to hit, while the overburdened communications needed to feed them were providing a target for guerrillas—it would have been much worse if these narrow mountain routes had been bombed from the air. In this state of stagnation, discontent was growing in the territory around them and among their native allies. Then the Abyssinian leaders came to their rescue by attempting a series of massed attacks, thus providing a target for machine-guns on the ground and overhead. In exploiting the Abyssinians' recoil, the Italian command turned their infantry masses into road-makers and relied for their own thrust on relatively small motorized spearheads, while mustard gas was sprayed to shield their own communications against the enemy's interference, and also to demoralize the troops and populated areas behind the enemy's front. The advance of these mobile columns was covered by a long-range and flexible barrage of air bombers, while their supplies were in part brought up by air transport.

It is significant that although the Italians were strategically on the offensive almost throughout the campaign, they combined it, almost as consistently, with the tactical defensive. In the four battles which mainly contributed to turn the scales of the war, and settle the fate of Abyssinia, the defeated side attempted most of the attacking. The first three, even Amba Aradam, seem to have been a tale of repeated Ethiopian assaults to forestall or stem the Italians' advance; and in the final battle the Emperor's army shattered itself against the Italians' fire-defence. Thus while the campaign superficially suggested that modern armament gives new power to the attack—at any rate where one side has a definite superiority of arms—its deeper lesson lies in the way the Italians profited from the power of modern defence, applied in a manœuvring advance.

The Abyssinian Campaign should have given the General Staffs of the world other cause for thought. It has shown the fallacy of their argument that machines are not a substitute for men—by which they mean the weight of the many, not the quality of the essential few. It has shown, more clearly even than the World War, that mass has become a dangerous encumbrance when the attempt is made to concentrate it on the fighting front. Under modern conditions, and especially the growing menace of air attack, the larger the army the weaker a country may prove in war. Technical quality counts, not drilled quantity.

4

The French Army

THE FRENCH ARMY HAS FOR LONG EXEMPLI-
fied the fallacy of the old standards of gauging strength.
If its total numbers were counted, it appeared the
"strongest" in Europe, apart from the Russian. That
idea was reinforced if trained reserves of men and stored
reserves of war material were reckoned. And the impression has thus been spread that the French Army
was, at any rate until recently, a serious potential threat
to Germany. But the numbers had small offensive meaning under modern conditions; a large proportion were
abroad; and most of the war material was old. Although
twenty-two tank battalions have been maintained in
France most of them were, and still are, equipped with
machines of the last war, slightly renovated. They are
slow machines, employed to help the infantry forward,
yet with a very limited obstacle-crossing capacity for
that purpose. The Army comprises twenty infantry divisions, five cavalry divisions, and five colonial infantry
divisions which serve as a "mobile force" ready for despatch to deal with trouble overseas.

The total "strength" of the French Army is some 640,-
000, but of these nearly 200,000 are serving in North
Africa and other colonies. Conscript service is still
nominally for one year, but contingents are now being
held for an extra year. This is due to the threat of the
German military expansion combined with the shrinkage of the annual contingent of young men reaching
military age (caused by the fall of the birth-rate during
the last war). The shrinkage, together with the need for
adequately trained personnel in the mechanized arms,
has also led the French to enlist an increased proportion
of long-service professional soldiers, who form a corps
of specialists. A maximum of 117,000 has been legally
sanctioned, although only some 80,000 have been obtained hitherto, as the terms have not been sufficiently
attractive. This element is one of several new factors
contributing to the transformation of the French Army.

Two recent visits to France afforded me the opportunity of renewing, after an interval of some eight years,
my acquaintance with that Army. They were also an
opportunity of gauging the trend of its military thought.
Such actual contact is apt to produce stronger impres-
sions than any perusal of a country's service papers. For
even in a country such as France, which has a great tradition of military literature, military ideas are no longer
expressed with the freedom of the eighteenth century:
that most vital age of military thought, when men like
Saxe, Bourcet and Guibert paved the way for the revolution in strategy which the young Napoleon Bonaparte
was able to achieve with the leverage of the Revolution.
Because of that age of fertilizing ideas, the intellectual

homage of every military student is due to France. Since then she has suffered as much as any country from the sterilization of thought which came with the increasing professionalization of armies. It is true that in the years preceding the World War, she could still produce a Colin and a Grouard, but such minds did not guide her strategy in 1914—as history too clearly tells. Nor did the shattering experiences of the war, which at least brought appreciation of the sober common sense of a Pétain, seem to succeed in breaking the fetters on thought even to the extent that was seen elsewhere. In France perhaps more than anywhere the subordination that must prevail in the sphere of action was extended into the sphere of conception, with a consequent barrenness. Orthodoxy was exalted to such a pitch that it became the most powerful of contraceptives.

Thus when I last saw the French Army it seemed to me almost the most backward in ideas among the armies of the Great Powers. After eight years for reflection upon the experience of the last war it showed small sign that reflection had borne fruit. Its horizon was bounded by 1918. If war should come again it apparently intended to resume where it had left off. That was better than the cry of "Back to 1914" which had echoed in some other armies during the years of reconstruction; but they had begun to move forward subsequently, if only in thought, whereas French thought had, in general, remained stationary, despite the bold leap into the future that was made in the immediate post-war utterances of some of the leading soldiers of France. The cause may have been that in France these original ideas were sprinkled from above, by generals who soon disappeared, whereas in Britain they were like springs welling up from below.

In French military doctrine and training all else was subordinated to the production of a great volume of fire, by methods that were as studiously deliberate as the rate of movement they promised. The best thing that could be said of the doctrine was that it recognized the importance of material factors, especially the effect of fire, and recanted the fallacious belief of 1914 that the unshielded will of the soldier was proof against bullets and shells. But it seemed to ignore the truth that fire is a means to movement, and that the effect is lost unless it can be followed up quickly. The division was still the profusely armed but complex organ of war-time pattern. The French seemed to have conceived of nothing more than the preservation of a powerful but rigid fighting machine, a machine which was likely to break down from its own internal friction if it should ever be called upon to make a prolonged advance or retirement. I could not help thinking that the French had renovated their steam-roller by fitting an extra roller, but had forgotten to consider its motive-power.

Since this visit, what I had heard from other observers had tended to confirm the impression. They spoke of the extreme deliberation of operations, of detail carried so far that it became an encumbrance. More recently, I had heard rumours of development, but not sufficient to prepare me for the change which I found.

By contrast with eight years earlier, it struck me as a remarkable evolution—much greater than our own in the

same period. And the development has been not only in
ideas but in application. If even to-day military thought
in France does not leap forward quite so boldly as among
the most progressive British soldiers, practical steps have
been larger.

Two cavalry divisions have been completely mechanized, mainly with armoured fighting vehicles, although
they have a proportion of "motor-dragoons" in light cars
and on motor-cycles. A heavy mechanized division is to
be created in 1937, to provide a still more powerful
punch, particularly for a counter-stroke against any hostile mechanized forces which might penetrate, by surprise, the fortified frontier. In addition, some ten infantry divisions have been motorized; their artillery is all
tractor-drawn, their infantry regiments are provided
with little armoured carriers for mortars, machine-guns,
and ammunition, and can themselves be moved by lorry
convoy. As regards supply, it is significant that the
French now consider the possibility of maintaining the
divisions at a much greater distance from railhead than
the British have yet contemplated.

The creation of these new-type formations, so different from the rest of the active forces, and from the
bulk army of mobilization, is naturally leading the
French towards a new picture of warfare. It tends to
resemble the vision which General von Seeckt and others
cast on the screen of the future during the years when
the German Army was being rebuilt, although modified
to suit the technical, geographical, and political conditions of France.

General mobilization is a process that works slowly in

putting an army into the field: so slowly indeed, that if mobilization and concentration were made as in 1914, the army would court the risk of never reaching the field. Air pressure on the congested traffic arteries might cause a premature collapse. Even at the best, an interval of a week or two must elapse before these forces can come into action. But the new-type formations, helped by their special composition as well as by their rail-free mobility, may be ready within a time that we commonly count in hours. To keep them in waiting while the bulk army was assembling would be a precarious discount of the time-factor, even if the enemy's action allowed the attempt.

Thus, in the new picture, the first phase of a war is fought out by the mobile forces together with the frontier garrisons. The second phase, of conflict between the mass forces, is provided for as a possibility—although some regard it as a doubtful one. Naturally, the picture is clearer in the minds of the younger men who are now rising to positions of influence than it is among those whose minds are filled with memories of how they conducted war in 1914–18. But the fact of this changing outlook is unmistakable, and it has a bearing on British military problems which deserves attention.

I have referred earlier to the modifications in the French picture produced by national conditions. They become most manifest in regard to the employment of the new-type formations. French thought revolves more than ever around the particular problem of safeguarding France against invasion—a problem essentially defensive. And French military thought inclines to share this tendency, certainly more than at times in the past. Thus the new-type formations seem to be visualized, above all, as a means of strengthening defence—by switching fire more quickly to a threatened spot and by developing a counter-offensive more promptly. To many there may be novelty in this "defensive" view of the value of mechanized forces. But it is justified on technical grounds. Despite the obvious increase of offensive power conferred by mechanized forces, the reinforcement of the defensive may well prove greater still, indirectly. On a long view, it might even be said that this has been the trend of the growing mechanization of war through the centuries.

From the contemporary point of view, it is politically as well as militarily significant that the French should be mainly concerned to fit the new development to their defensive problem—of resisting the invasion which they apprehend. I had the impression that their ideas on this aspect were much clearer than on any wider aspects. That reflection made me cast my mind across the frontier; I thought of those who in Germany have been haunted by fear of invasion—a feeling that is widespread if not so deep-rooted as in France. If they could have shared in my contact with the actual scope of French military ideas, their fears might have been allayed. Statesmanship may suffer as much by failing to grasp what soldiers are thinking as by ignoring public opinion. The former is the more stable of the two.

It was ironically said of the Kellogg Pact that its effect was not to abolish war, but merely the declaration of war. So also, in the world to-day, "defence" is a conventional euphemism which embraces offence. The embrace, however, may be willing or reluctant. If one follows the trend of military thought in the different countries one may get as shrewd an idea of the predominant attitude as in following the more fluctuating course of policy. To gauge it one must go beneath the surface: for the offensive is so much a part of the military tradition, and so much more appealing than the defensive to the soldierly spirit. On the surface of the training grounds, attack exercises predominate. Indeed, to a casual observer, the armies of the least warlike countries might well seem the most belligerent—since the more shadowy a country's military problem, the more probable that its army will spend its time in practising the type of action it is unlikely to fulfil. Armed forces are most ruled by force of custom when dangers are least concrete. Training tends to become a truer expression of purpose when political conditions produce concrete possibilities.

The fact that the French Army shows a firmer grasp of defensive contingencies than of offensive ones would seem a reasonable clue to the attitude of its leaders. The preponderance of the defensive finds expression in the frontier fortifications to which so much of their money and attention have been devoted in recent years. That newly fortified line, for the most part·running just inside the frontier, has been widely discussed.

It consists, as is well known, of a chain of forts and casemates—the proportions varying not only according to the ground but to the money available. The "forts" (according to details which have appeared) themselves consist of a mushroom-like cluster of concrete casemates linked by underground galleries; these lead to the living quarters, magazines, and power stations which serve each cluster, and are likewise buried deep. The sector first constructed was from Longuyon, opposite Luxembourg, to the Vosges; this covered Metz and the Briey industrial area, although a gap was originally left on either side of the Sarre River between St. Avold and Bitche, where a succession of streams parallel with the frontier helped to form a natural barrier. Subsequently this gap has been filled, in part at least, and the chain of fortifications has been extended along the Rhine to the Swiss frontier, to supplement this river barrier. The defence of the approaches through Belgium and Belgian Luxembourg has also been taken in hand, work being carried out along the line of the frontier towards Maubeuge and Lille. According to plan, the intervals in the chain were to be covered by the interlacing fire of the casemates, but could also be more substantially filled by field entrenchments and the whole covered by wire entanglements. This, I believe, is now being done. And the fortified chain is to be extended to Dunkirk in the north, and to the Jura in the south, along the Swiss frontier.

Such a fortified line, although better designed, naturally lacks the depth of protection afforded by the vast trench systems which developed in the war. Stronger in meeting the first shock, it is intended to gain time rather than to be a final barrier. It is, above all, a shock-absorber, to cover the process of mobilization. Its effectiveness thus depends on the adequacy and readiness of the forces which normally garrison it, and on the promptness with which support can be given. The main danger lies in a surprise attack which might overwhelm a sector before the emergency was realized; a further danger now on the horizon is a penetration of the intervals by mechanized forces, which might disregard the forts or leave them to be "mopped up" by a second wave of invaders.

It is for this reason that the French are so concerned with the new risks of the *attaque brusquée*. Some of them visualize the possibility of hostile mechanized forces crossing the old demilitarized zone by a swift bound during a single night and delivering their stroke early next morning. All of them now appear to realize, from this point of view at least, the great acceleration of the *tempo* of warfare which modern developments foreshadow.

The technical conditions of warfare have tended more and more to enhance the advantage of the defence, and to discount the numerical superiority which an invader may possess. Thereby they have much diminished the chances of successful invasion. In consequence, however, they have largely concentrated the remaining chances in the possibility of achieving an initial surprise. Unless a decisive advantage is gained in a short time, the paralysis of the offensive is likely to be established more firmly than ever—unless the endurance of the defender should be undermined by pressure from behind, through the internal collapse of the country and the cessation of supplies.

In 1914 a fortnight elapsed after mobilization before the advance of the main armies began. An aggressor who nowadays waited so long would have a poor prospect of gaining a decision. If this knowledge, when assimilated, may prove a powerful deterrent to aggression, it inevitably tends to focus the thought of a would-be aggressor on the ways of achieving a short-time penetration by surprise. There are some in France who fear it so much, and become so absorbed in contemplation of their own risks, that they hardly pause to ask whether the possible invaders have the organization or the means to execute it. The General Staff, with their superior sources of information, preserve a firmer grasp of existing possibilities without overlooking the future.

Meantime the problem of immediate concern is to adapt their own organization to the current of changing conditions. One need is to remodel the mobilization scheme so as to produce an effective force in support of the frontier garrisons in the shortest possible time—a time that we must now count in hours rather than in days. That mobilization scheme must also take account of the new risks threatened by hostile air attack during the main process of mobilization and concentration. Concentration must not spell congestion. It should be in the current but not on the surface. Rail and road movements must be more flexible, and the whole must be more distributed.

The other need is to develop mechanization as a means of saving time in arrival and intervention. The fortified region itself is garrisoned by units of varying composition which are "hand-made" to suit the sector allotted to them; they can be brought up to strength at short notice with reservists drawn from the neighbouring district. But for the prompt support of the region, and for

manœuvre based on this pivot, mobile formations are
necessary. The need is now being met.

As a start, the 4th Cavalry Division was transformed
into a light mechanized division, and the 5th is now being
converted. The fighting part of the division consists of
what are called *auto-mitrailleuses*—light and medium
armoured vehicles on tracks which we should describe
as tanks—cavalry tanks. They are all fast machines. The
other part is of mixed composition to fit its mixed role of
reconnoitring the enemy and seizing "stepping stones";
it has a regiment of *auto-mitrailleuses*, at present on
wheels, and a regiment of *dragons portés*—cavalrymen
mounted in light and handy unarmoured vehicles that
are capable of moving across country. Each has a strong
infusion of motor-cyclists—a type of the troops which
the French have developed notably.

In the infantry divisions which have been motorized
the artillery is entirely tractor-drawn—light and medium
lorries being used for the purpose. Compared with our
own mechanized artillery it has a marked advantage for
strategic road movements, owing to the fact that the
guns are carried on a low trailer, from which they can
be dismounted in half a minute on reaching the battlefield. The use of these trailers, lifting the gun-wheels off
the ground, enables the artillery to travel long distances
at speeds up to 40 m.p.h. without damaging the more
delicate mechanism of the gun.

Chenillettes—armoured carriers somewhat similar to
the British Carden-Loyds—are being introduced in these
divisions for the transport of the infantry mortar, machine-gun, and ammunition. Motorization is at present

only partial in the infantry, although they are commonly embussed for long moves. But several regiments have been completely motorized for the trial of a new organization.

Here one may interpolate that the tank units, as distinct from those of *auto-mitrailleuses*, still belong to the infantry arm. This is partly explained by their low speed, but is also due to the fact that the French have never gone back to the belief that attacking infantry, in face of machine-guns, could dispense with armoured support. Realization of the difficulties of supplying the artillery with sufficient ammunition for the creeping barrages of the last war has also tended to emphasize the need for tanks. Where employed, a section to a company is allotted to aid each infantry battalion. Twenty battalions of so-called light tanks are maintained at home, but most of them are still equipped with renovated war-time machines; only a few have been provided with the newer type Renaults which weigh 11 tons (their armour being of 30 millimetre thickness) and have a maximum speed of 11 m.p.h. There is also one independent tank battalion, the embryo of the new heavy mechanized division. The monster 70-ton tanks which were introduced some years back did not give satisfaction, and the French are still looking for an efficient heavy tank of rather less weight; but a large medium tank of some 25 tons is said to be now in production, and a heavy tank of 37 tons under trial.

The development of mechanization in the army is creating fresh problems of personnel. Thanks to the economy of time achieved by the present system of training, and to the admirable simplification of drill, the ordinary infantry attain a remarkably high standard in proportion to the shortness of their service. But it is more difficult to provide adequately trained personnel for the mechanized supporting weapons and the mechanized services in general. For these needs, the French are tending to rely on the increased professional element, which now forms a corps of specialists. Here, however, a fresh problem arises—not only how to recruit sufficient numbers but how to recruit a sufficiently high grade of man. The trend of modern warfare emphasizes the importance of finding a solution. For the unskilled man, in the services as in industry, is losing his utility. Quality outweighs quantity on the modern battlefield.

5

The British Army

THE BRITISH ARMY AS VOTED BY PARLIAMENT consists of some 168,000 officers and men, and of this total 38,000 are serving abroad. But a further 57,000, stationed in India, belong to it, although while serving there they are not paid for by the British public. Thus nearly half the Regular Army is employed on foreign service even in quiet times. The troops at home are organized in five infantry divisions—one less than before the war, owing to the disbandment of the Irish regiments. Behind the Regular Army there is the Territorial Army, composed of civilian soldiers who spend a fortnight annually in camp, besides training in the evenings at their local drill hall. Its establishment is 203,000 but its strength at present is under 150,000; it has been recently rising, however, after years of decline.

The British Army has many points of difference from those of the Continent. While they are large, it is small; while they are raised by conscription, it depends on voluntary enlistment; while they have short-service, it has long-service—seven years is the normal; while they are raised from all classes, it is drawn from the poor.

In the past it largely depended for filling its ranks on those who were too uneducated and resourceless to find better-paid employment; and while the officers were drawn from the other social extreme it was a family principle that the Army was the vocation of those sons who were not likely to shine in other professions. If there has been some change in this basis, it persists sufficiently to be a handicap in days when the trend of warfare places an increasing premium on intelligence. Moreover, its social tradition tends to make the British Army highly conservative. On the other hand, it has in a measure escaped the narrow professionalism which marks some of the Continental officer corps through the fact that so many of its officers had independent means, and also through the variety of its service.

This brings us to the greatest difference between the British and the Continental Armies. While their primary purpose is the defence of their own country—a euphemism which embraces the attack on a neighbouring country—that of the British Army is the defence of, and maintenance of order in, the British Empire. These duties have governed its basic organization. In the nineteenth century it became so predominantly a colonial service army as to become quite unfit, both quantitatively and qualitatively, to face the contingency of a European war. Thus in 1868 Mr. Cardwell, then Secretary of State for War, established the principle that there should be a battalion at home for each one maintained abroad. Under the "Cardwell System" the units at home provide drafts for those on foreign service, and the regiment, instead of being a fighting organization as in other armies, consists of linked home and foreign battalions, which never serve together but merely interchange officers and men.

Besides finding drafts for the overseas garrisons, the home army has also to provide a potential expeditionary force, either to act as an Imperial fire-brigade in guarding a serious outbreak in the overseas territories, or as a contribution to the collective forces ranged against an aggressive European power. This last role, if deeply rooted in British history, was only revived a few years before 1914, when an expeditionary force of six divisions was erected as part of the Haldane Reforms. If its size was puny compared with the armies that the Continental powers could mobilize, and its equipment barely as good as theirs, it had a definite qualitative advantage through longer training; from its hard experience in the Boer War it had learnt the value of markmanship, and thus in 1914 its volume of aimed rifle-fire took the Germans by surprise and created the impression that it possessed quantities of machine-guns. This fire capacity gave it a weight beyond its numbers, and, combined with the natural "sticking-power" of the British soldier, enabled it to renew its traditional record in repelling attacks. But it showed less aptitude for the offensive, and as its numbers grew through expansion on a national scale, it tended to expand them prodigally but unprofitably. In the tank, however, it produced the most important new offensive weapon of the war; and in the last phase this weapon, together with the improved technique which developed with experience, helped it to gain distinction in forcing entrenched positions.

After the war Britain gave up conscription, and went

back from her war-time army of millions to one even smaller than in 1914. Yet in one respect this post-war army took the lead among the European powers. Instead of being content to copy Continental ideas and practice, a new school of military thought arose which went back to an older tradition and thence went forward, via its war-time experience with tanks, to a fresh conception of mobile mechanized warfare. These ideas, although at first regarded as heresy or fantasy, gradually made headway and eventually won acceptance. They also focussed the attention of the military world on the experiments carried out by the British Army, and have now borne fruit in the general mechanization of armies.

But in this translation of theory into actual equipment Britain herself has fallen behind. The political desire to postpone measures of rearmament, the inherent conservatism of the senior military chiefs, the inelastic requirements of the Cardwell System and the retarding power of India—these are some of the factors that have put a brake on material progress. Another is the characteristic British tendency to seek technical perfection instead of going into production as soon as it has found something that will be fairly effective. The result is that the chief foreign armies have already a far larger quantity of modern mechanized troops when Britain, despite her much smaller army, is only beginning its general re-equipment.

It was not until the end of 1935 that the War Office reached the point of embarking on a big scheme of reorganization and modernization. The cavalry were to be mechanized, part being equipped with light tanks and part, provisionally, with a new kind of light motor vehicle, with large wheels and oversize tires, that can travel across country—it looks like an adaption of the Irish jaunting car, the seating being so designed that each man on board can jump out easily, and go instantly into action on foot. It is intended to create a Mobile Division—to take the place of the old Cavalry Division—which will consist of two mechanized Cavalry Brigades, mainly composed of light tanks, with a Tank Brigade (the British Army has only one) attached and detachable. At the same time twenty-six battalions of infantry out of a hundred and thirty-six are being converted into mechanized machine-gun units. It was originally intended to have one of these battalions in each infantry brigade, but it has now been decided to employ them as divisional and corps troops, while the infantry brigade will be reduced to three "rifle" battalions. These, being relieved of their heavier and more complex weapons, will be easier to handle and to train, while their manœuvring power is being improved by the motorization of their transport. Although called "rifle" battalions, each of them will have fifty-two light machine-guns—one in each little section of half a dozen men—thus increasing their firepower.

The past two years have thus been marked by some definite steps towards the modernization of the Army. Hitherto the post-war period had seen much activity of ideas—there is abundant evidence that British military thought has for the first time commanded the attention of, and blazed the trail for, the armies of the world. That development of ideas produced in turn a growth of practical experiments in mechanization, tactics, and organization. But the experiments had less consistency and tenacity than the ideas—sometimes they were ill-planned; sometimes discontinued because of some contrary current, and then renewed after a needless loss of time and experience. Meantime the Army as a whole went on almost unchanged—in a pattern that might serve for Imperial policing—with some improvised help from motor transport—but became ever less suited to the conditions of modern warfare. So long as money was lacking, and no foreign danger was on the immediate horizon, the authorities preferred to postpone modernization in order to keep intact the number of men and of units. They might have reorganized the Army on a smaller scale and newer pattern; but this alternative course was hindered by the system of financial control, by the Cardwell System, by mistrust of what the "politicians" might do with money thus saved for re-equipment, and by a natural reluctance to embark on changes of uncertain issue. On the existing scale of units, the margin of money available for new equipment was inevitably small. Experiments continued, but no serious attempt to apply their results was feasible until an increase in the total money became likely.

That change of prospect took place in 1935. The sum available for "warlike stores" was doubled—being raised to £4,500,000 (out of total estimates of £43,500,000). Although nearly half of this had to be devoted to the replenishment of ammunition reserves, the balance enabled considerable progress to be made in providing units with mechanized transport and other up-to-date equipment.

As a light machine-gun the Czechoslovakian "Bren"

was adopted, and arrangements made for its production in England, to supersede the war-time Lewis gun. The Army also heard that it was, at last, to be equipped with anti-tank guns: two types were adopted—one a "hand gun" and the other a heavier weapon, but both have a penetrative power much higher than those formerly tried. With the mechanization of the infantry mortars, the task of giving close support to the infantry was handed over to this weapon, in place of the light howitzer. At the same time, the artillery support, and its fluidity, were increased by the conversion of the "light" (formerly "pack") artillery brigades into additional mechanized field brigades. The cavalry were also the subject of an experiment in mechanization, a squadron of the 3rd Hussars having their horses replaced by a new type of light motor vehicle, capable of travelling across country, and from which the men could jump out instantly.

The progress of the Army was thus mainly directed towards improving the general mobility of the older arms—in contrast to the latest trend abroad, where efforts were being made to create a number of "mechanized" divisions in the full sense, basically composed of armoured fighting vehicles. In the British Army the one Tank Brigade continued in existence, but was not yet completely equipped with up-to-date light tanks and had no modern medium tanks.

The Territorial Army was still left waiting for any general modernization of its equipment or organization, but it was given an increased responsibility in the defence of this country against the danger of air attack.

Part of the new anti-aircraft units required for this purpose were to be formed by the conversion of existing infantry units. A number of battalions in London were already converted to anti-aircraft artillery or searchlights before the end of the year.

At the end of the year came the announcement of the first really large steps in Army reorganization since the war. One was the mechanization of the cavalry. This had been decided on in preference to their reduction and the expansion of the Royal Tank Corps. If this was rather hard on the newer arm, which had borne the burden of developing the means and methods of mechanized warfare, it enabled the preservation of the Cavalry tradition, general and regimental. Some doubt must remain, until experience proves the contrary, as to the ability of horse-minded soldiers to become mechanically minded and to get as much out of their machines as a corps who are natural enthusiasts for machinery. But the mechanization of the cavalry was at any rate in significant, if somewhat ironical, contrast to the fervent declarations of continued belief in the value of cavalry which the spokesman of the War Office had made in Parliament only two or three years before. Cavalry, if viewed with a sense of reality, have been ghosts on the battle-field ever since they were reduced, by modern fire, to dismounted action as a normal course on meeting opposition. And now that any kind of troops can be moved in motor-vehicles, the distinction between cavalry and infantry is becoming artificial, except in the case of cavalry who are converted into armoured car or light tank regiments. These alone retain the basic historical characteristics of the cavalryman—*the man who fights mounted*. The tankman and the airman are the true heirs of "cavalry" in their mode of action.

Early in 1936 further decisions were taken towards the modernization of the infantry. They involved the complete mechanization of its first line transport, horse-limbers being superseded by the new 15-cwt. Morris trucks, while even the officers' chargers were to be replaced by light cars or motor-cycles.

In addition, troop-carrying companies were to be created as part of the Royal Army Service Corps, equipped with motor coaches or lorries sufficient to move the men of a whole infantry brigade. There was to be one of these troop-carrying companies for each infantry division. Their provision promised to increase the mobility of the infantry, while further increasing efficiency by economizing energy. Hitherto the value of the mechanization of first line transport had been curtailed by the fact that the bulk of the personnel still had to march.

The new divisional organization—with its three infantry brigades of smaller size and its heavier infantry weapons under divisional control—is expected to improve manageability and to diminish road congestion, while allowing a more flexible power of concentrating extra fire support at the vital points. This accords with the principle already adopted with the artillery, wherein the artillery permanently allotted to the division is kept on a minimum scale, while its potential support is on a maximum scale. Just as the increased proportion of "army" artillery enables the divisions which have the harder nuts to crack to be heavily reinforced for the moment, so the infantry brigades can be treated similarly in giving them machine-gun support in accord with their need.

The reorganized rifle battalions, divested of their heavy machine-guns will consist of four homogeneous companies, each with twelve of the new Bren guns. The new infantry organization constitutes an official recognition of the growing value of the light machine-gun in modern warfare compared with the rifle. It has raised the question whether the rifle should be discarded.

Recognizing the limitations of the rifle as a factor in modern battle, some soldiers consider that it is now only of use for hill warfare and sniping. Others who agree with them in principle would not go so far. A rifle can be a deadly weapon in the hands of a man who is both an expert shot and skilled in the use of ground: it can be used, and one has seen it used, most effectively in stalking hostile machine-guns. Yet to concede its value as a fine weapon in expert hands does not affect the basic point. For we cannot expect the bulk of the men who are recruited for the Regular infantry to attain the necessary expertness. It is a still more improbable assumption that the mass of the Territorial Army, or the men who are hastily raised in war, will become experts. Thus there is a strong case for re-examining the foundations of tactical power in the light of modern conditions.

It is uneconomic to send into action more men than can contribute effectively to the issue. More men merely mean more loss without compensating profit. If it were not for ammunition supply, one man would suffice, and two would be ample, for handling each light machine-gun: as mechanized means of carrying ammunition on the battle-field develop so the uneconomic call for more human carriers will disappear. Here it is not without significance to recall that in the Palestine campaign Lawrence, a most expert rifle-shot, came to discard the rifle for a stripped light automatic as his personal weapon —his camel served as the carrier, enabling him to make the Lewis gun a one-man weapon. To send into action, as at present, seven men with each light machine-gun is certainly uneconomic as a general rule. Two would be enough where extra ammunition can be brought up easily in a carrier; even where it could not, three men to aid the light machine-gunner could carry as many magazines as the present six men if they were relieved of their encumbering rifles. For close quarter fighting an automatic pistol would suffice: a "gangster" gun might perhaps be still better.

There are many occasions in war when "economic tactics" would suggest that only two men should go forward with the section's light machine-gun; the others being kept under cover, to go up later. In certain conditions—for example, at night and in other forms of obscurity, an increase of man-power in proportion to weapon-power is desirable. Even here it is questionable whether the present scale is not uneconomic. A smaller section would be less of a target, while its higher controllability would add to its effective strength. Moreover, the apparent reduction would be further offset by an increase in the number of units.

* * * * * * *

The manufacture of all the new equipment required for the British Army, as it is now being mechanized, is likely to take some years. Meantime the successive emergencies in Egypt and Palestine during 1935 and 1936 have stripped the home army of equipment and men, leaving the expeditionary force a skeleton. This state has strengthened the case of those who argue that the home army should be designed for use as a mobile Imperial Reserve, not as a potential field army for the Continent. Some who hold this view would concede the possible value of employing a small but highly mechanized force in suitable circumstances, where its quality might turn the scales, while doubting the wisdom of any large-scale participation in a Continental land struggle. Others would prefer that Britain definitely eschewed the idea of playing a part in Continental warfare, leaving to the Air Force any such intervention if it should be called for by her obligations.

6

The Rearmament of Britain

THE APPEARANCE AND ATMOSPHERE OF ENG-
land show but a slight reflection of the armament race
now in progress throughout Europe. There is none of
the bustle of military preparations which is so manifest
on the Continent. The landscape is not coloured by uni-
forms. But unobtrusively there is a considerable measure
of activity. The most noticeable sign, perhaps, is the
number of new military aerodromes—there are forty
more than at the end of 1934. Some of the great motor
factories, too, show large extensions for the building of
aircraft. The British Air Force is fast, if not furiously,
expanding to a formidable scale, while the other forces
are more gradually acquiring a new complexion. These
developments, however, will take time—and Britain has
much leeway to make up. Meantime her defence problems have developed faster.

The conquest of the air has laid low her old sea-wall
of seclusion, and brought her into uncomfortably close
neighbourhood with the Continent. The rebirth of Germany in arms has affected her situation indirectly even
more than directly, because of its impetus to the general

expansion of forces, which works to the widespread disadvantage of a scattered empire which has so many
points of contact with the domains of other nations. And
her situation, from a military point of view, is more complicated than it was before 1914. She was committed by
post-war engagements to a generalized effort to resist
any aggression against other countries, and to a more
specific guarantee in Western Europe: although recent
events have loosened the former tie it remains a potential
source of entanglement.

Meantime old friends have become estranged, while
becoming more formidable as military powers: with this
development goes an appetite for new territory which,
accentuated by their martial tastes, threatens a clash of
interests. Italy lies athwart Britain's main trade-route to
the East, through the Mediterranean and the Red Sea.
Japan is encroaching on its eastern extremity, thus imposing a two-way stretch on British resources which is
all the more of a strain owing to the increased length of
her communications and their intermediate susceptibility
to pressure. And there is the still more uncomfortable
possibility of a new combination of pressure at the point
where Britain's Mediterranean and Cape routes converge.
Even when goodwill prevails it is not easy for countries,
in which an essentially different form of government
and basis of society exists, to reconcile their respective
aims. Britain's coasts and causeways are now lapped by
totalitarian tides.

After the World War the British forces were rapidly
reduced, and the country returned to the traditional system of voluntary enlistment which it had temporarily

abandoned when the war was in its second year. The Army was brought back to less than its pre-war size, which had naturally been much smaller than the conscript armies of the Continent. The Air Force, which had been built up to the highest level of any by the end of the war, was reduced to a skeleton—from 185 squadrons to 28, of which only three were available for the defence of the home country. With the Washington Treaty Britain gave up her long-standing claim to predominance on the seas, and agreed to a condition of parity with the next strongest naval power.

In 1922 the Geddes Committee, appointed to consider economies in national expenditure, went so far as to suggest reducing the Air Force to a mere eight squadrons. The older services—conservative in a double sense—were more than content to see their young sister's allowance cut down if it saved a little more for themselves. But a check was imposed after strong Press criticism initiated in *The Times* by General Groves, a former member of the Air Staff. And just afterwards a state of tension developed with Britain's former allies, when the French marched into the Ruhr to impose their will on conquered Germany. The British, making plain their dislike of this invasion, felt a strong sense of personal discomfort when they awoke to the fact that a considerable part of France's 126 air squadrons were assembled within reach of their own coast.

The outcome was the announcement by Mr. Baldwin in 1923 that, apart from overseas requirements, "British air power must include a home-defence force of sufficient strength adequately to protect us against air attack by the strongest air force within striking distance of this country". He stated that the force was to consist of 52 squadrons, to be created as quickly as possible. The expansion started promptly, but was checked in 1926 when still a long way from completion. Three years later the official spokesman of the Air Ministry disclosed to Parliament that Britain had sunk to fifth place among the world's air powers. Yet the incomplete programme was again suspended, first to meet the economic crisis, and then to meet the hopes of a general limitation raised by the Disarmament Conference which assembled in 1932. During these years all service expenditure had been steadily pared down. If the Navy suffered least, as the favourite child of British tradition, the modernization of its capital ships was put off longer than in either the United States or Japan, while its own youngest and least cherished child, the Fleet Air Arm, had to be content with crumbs. The Army, faced with a shrinking purse, conservatively preferred to save on new equipment rather than at the expense of historic units. Although younger brains had given the British Army a technical lead in the means and methods of mechanized warfare, to the older heads modernization seemed less important than the maintenance of infantry numbers. In this endeavour they even allowed the reserves of ammunition to sink below what would be needed if the Army had to take the field. Nevertheless the Army and Navy together were taking six times as much money as the Air Force from the total allotted for defence—a little over a hundred million pounds a year. The disproportion gave a curious reflection to the Government's admission that:

"The advent of the air weapon has lost us our age-long security as an island nation, and has left the greatest city in the world more open to the dangers of air attacks than any of the other capitals in Europe."

This prolonged curtailment of expenditure on the forces, while fostered by the urge for economy, was justified by the Government's formal assurance to the heads of the services that no major war need be anticipated within a period of ten years ahead. The ruling was renewed annually—until it lapsed, and the country suddenly found itself confronted with the possibility of a war within much less than ten years.

The strengthening and re-equipment of the British defences continued to be postponed so long as some hope, if a diminishing hope, hung on the Disarmament Conference—although well before this the Continental powers and Japan had obviously begun rearmament. The pace of this quickened with the advent of the Nazi government in Germany, and its unconcealed measures. Eventually the British Government took account of the danger and made a detailed examination of the state of their own forces. The result awakened them to many deficiencies—and the impression would have been worse if they had studied the technical trend of modern warfare enough to gauge the more serious qualitative defects. Even as it was, their confession of national deficiencies contrasted vividly with the complacent assurance that they had dished out to Parliament year after year in answer to a few critical voices.

The immediate result of this enquiry was that in July, 1934, the Government adopted a five-year programme for increasing the Air Force, and raising the home defence part of it to seventy-five squadrons. They were soon led to quicken their step, and shorten the time of their programme, owing to evidence of Germany's rapid development in the air and the expansion of other air forces. Early in 1935, France had 1650 first line machines, Italy 1050, and Russia over 2000, while Britain had 1020, of which 688 were at home. By the end of the year she now aimed to have 1180 altogether, and in 1936 to have 1310. Ground defences against air attacks were also increased. Until then London alone had any such defences, and they were provided by merely two skeleton brigades of Territorial anti-aircraft artillery and searchlight units—composed of citizen volunteers, who go to camp for a fortnight a year and do occasional evenings' training during the rest of the year. It was decided to break up two Territorial infantry divisions and convert them into anti-aircraft troops, to man a long belt of defence running from the south coast up the east coast, so that it would cover the north country industrial areas as well as London. This conversion is not yet completed, nor the provision of the necessary guns and searchlights. A research committee of scientists has also been formed to study new means of countering attacks.

At the same time that this immediate defence of Great Britain was thus taken in hand, extra money was provided for beginning the modernization of the Army and Navy, although their actual size was not to be appreciably increased. Indeed the Army found difficulty in recruiting up to the existing strength of approximately 200,000, and by the end of the year was 10,000 short.

Although £4,000,000 was added to the Army vote—a 10 per cent increase—a large part of this was absorbed by the need to make up depleted reserves of ammunition, and barely half a million was allotted for modern mechanized equipment. With the Navy an increase was restricted by Treaty conditions, and the construction of new ships was limited to normal replacement: it included three new cruisers. But during recent years the already difficult problem of guarding the immense length of the trade-routes with naval forces smaller than before the war, has been complicated by the development of submarines and of torpedo-carrying speed-boats in several of the Continental navies, notably those of Italy and France. On top of this looms the menace both to merchant shipping and their naval guardians, as well as to the ports on which they depend, that comes from shore-based aircraft—anywhere those trade-routes are within the ever-growing range of the air-weapon.

The new programme had barely been decided when a new series of shocks caused its upward revision. In March, 1935, Germany startled the world with the announcement of her reintroduction of conscription and the formation of an army of thirty-six divisions, or some 600,000 men—fifty per cent larger than the French. It was followed by Hitler's intimation, to the British ministers who had gone over to Berlin for friendly negotiations, that Germany already possessed parity in the air with Britain and was aiming at parity with France—which meant a superiority to the prospective British air force. If there was some doubt about his first assertion, his second was plain. And a fortnight later the German

Government disclosed that it was again building submarines.

The sequel was that in May, 1935, the British Government decided to raise its own intended air strength by
fifty squadrons, and to have a home defence force of
1500 first line machines within the next two years. This
involved the construction of an additional thirty air
stations beyond the eighteen new ones already planned,
and also the training of 2500 new pilots as well as of
20,000 other personnel. Although still hoping for any
agreed limitation, the British Government was no longer
content to let preparedness wait on hope.

But the process of expanding the Air Force and reno-
vating the Army was to suffer an unforeseen complica-
tion; it came from Italy's invasion of Abyssinia and the
tension this act of aggression caused with Britain. As the
chief upholder of the League Covenant, she was naturally the target if sanctions should culminate in war. If
she was better placed than any of the other powers to
hinder the despatch of Italian forces to Abyssinia, should
the League's intervention go so far, her own communications were also exposed to possible interruption by
Italy. A sudden realization of this awkward position
(which is discussed at more length in Chapter 9) led
the British fleet to leave its Mediterranean base at Malta,
which lay close to the Italian air bases, and move to the
far end of the Mediterranean. At the same time the military garrison needed strengthening. But the position in
Egypt, also, became precarious in view of Italy's increase
of force in Libya; the assembly there of mechanized divisions and powerful bombing squadrons was an obvious

threat to the security of Egypt and the new harbours of the British fleet. It led to a hasty despatch of air and army units thither, which imposed a severe strain on existing British resources. It temporarily upset the expansion of the Air Force by taking away the experienced officers and N.C.O.'s who were needed as instructors for the newly recruited pilots and mechanics. Although the Army sent barely the equivalent of one division, out of the nominal five maintained at home, the rest of the army had to be scraped of equipment in order to make that detachment an effective fighting force. All the modern type tanks, a mere hundred or so, were sent out, leaving the home forces to carry on with long obsolete machines, supplemented by ordinary light trucks masquerading as tanks, until the manufacture of war material could catch up with the needs that had too long been neglected. The available stocks of mechanized transport, wireless sets, and many other kinds of modern equipment, were almost as badly drained. The whole army at home was left bare of what it needed for war until manufacture could overtake deficiency.

The emergency revealed not only the shortage of men and material but a failure to make adequate arrangements beforehand. Hasty improvisation had to make good the absence of plans. The impression produced by these deficiencies, coupled with the uncertain state of service opinion on various technical issues, such as the effect of aircraft against warships, raised doubts whether the Government, in deciding upon measures of rearmament, had any clear picture of their aim. There was widespread anxiety lest the increasing outlay of money should fail of its purpose through faulty distribution; lest it was being governed merely by the endeavour to satisfy the demands of the three services, and based on a compromise between their separate interests, instead of being laid out on a fore-thoughtful plan. That anxiety found voice in *The Times*, which urged the need of viewing defence as a whole, and co-ordinating the activities of the three services as well as their supplies. This lead was supported by a growing volume of authoritative opinion, which included the testimony of several former service chiefs to the limitations of the existing system and its tendency to work by mere compromise. The proposal to develop a more powerful organ of co-ordination was strongly resisted in some quarters, but the Government eventually yielded to the weight of public opinion and in March, 1936, appointed a Minister for the Co-ordination of Defence, as well as three permanent, if junior, members to the Joint Planning Committee, at which the representatives of the three services meet. The Minister was not to be in charge of a department, but would act as the Prime Minister's deputy on the Committee of Imperial Defence, preside when necessary at the meetings of the Chiefs of Staff of the three services, and would also be in supreme charge of the supply organization and industrial planning. This was a step forward, if it did not go as far as was desirable: there was a danger that the new Minister might become too absorbed with the problems of providing the fighting services with equipment to have time for adjusting and combining their respective plans.

Sub-committees by the dozen have been set up to deal

with the different items of munition supply, with the provision of raw material and its manufacture, with man-power, food-supply, grain storage, as well as with such questions as the protection of merchant shipping, the development of anti-aircraft. defence, and precautions for the protection of the civilian population in air raids. A detailed survey has been made of the industrial field, to examine and clarify the material, operative and technical resources of the country. Hundreds of engineering firms have been inspected to see whether their plant is adaptable to munition production in war-time. Production for present needs, however, has been delayed by lack of the necessary machine-tools and gauges. The maintenance of the population itself is an even more complex problem. Two-thirds of the food required is at present imported from overseas—a total of some 50,000 tons a day. Agricultural production has been increased about 14 per cent in the last few years, and the country could be self-supporting in potatoes, eggs, vegetables and milk. But this is not possible with meat and cereals. In Britain there are, at any particular moment, only about six to twelve weeks' stocks of some of the main kinds of foodstuffs required. The renewed portents of war have reawakened the British people to the risks they run through their dependence on imported food, and consequently on the sea-routes by which those essential supplies are brought. It is this realization which, more than any threat from a specific quarter, has impelled the British Government to hasten the repair and expansion of its forces. It has also governed the direction of their main effort.

With the Air Force the interruption caused by the Mediterranean emergency was soon overcome, if not overtaken. The production of new types of machines, of much higher performance and greater range, has been speeded up so much that they are being delivered long before the date originally contemplated. The intended strength of the force at home has also been raised to 1750 first line aircraft, exclusive of the Fleet Air Arm, which is to be increased to at least 450 machines. The creation of the new squadrons, however, has been slower. Of the 72 which were to be raised by the end of March, 1937—to make a home defence total of 124—only about 26 will now be complete, with a further 22 formed on a one-flight basis. The remainder should be formed, if not at full strength, by the late summer. With the Navy, which had a relatively lesser problem, the rate of construction has been quickened to the extent that some of the new ships are expected to be ready nearly half a year earlier than the scheduled time. Five of the new class of 9000-ton cruisers are expected to be ready within the next year: they have a speed of 32 knots and an armament of twelve 6-inch guns, as well as eight 4-inch anti-aircraft guns. Similar progress is being made with the building of destroyers, while two new 35,000-ton battleships were laid down in January 1937, with three more to follow shortly. And the completion of the Singapore Base is being hastened. Last winter the Government decided to raise the cruiser strength from 50 to 70—the number which has for years been claimed as a necessary minimum by those directly concerned with the defence of the sea-communications: in 1914 there were 125 cruisers, new and old, available.

The situation is less comforting in regard to the deficiencies of the Army. The belated official acceptance of modernization and mechanization has caught its munition plants in a state of inadequacy for large-scale production, and a shortage of skilled labour has aggravated the difficulty. Even to-day it lacks any anti-tank guns, any modern light machine-guns, any assault tanks, any fast medium tanks that are fit for war. The motorization of its transport will take some time to complete. A new light machine-gun, the Bren, has been adopted to replace the wartime weapons that are still in use, and deliveries are expected to begin late in 1937. Some of the new anti-tank guns and anti-tank rifles may be available earlier. But the Territorial Army is even worse off and will have to wait longer.

A realization of the defective state of the Army has helped to give a new emphasis to an old theory—that Britain, even if she cannot avoid entanglement in Continental issues, should at least eschew the idea of landing an army on the Continent. A small field force from Britain, inevitably late in arrival, would seem to have little chance of influencing the issue or retrieving any advantage which an invader might gain by surprise in the first days of a new war; and the necessary peace-time preparations for its despatch to foreign ports are difficult to make without causing offence. By contrast, the air force could act from its own shores and could intervene in the first hours. The promise of such help would be more comfort to a threatened neighbour, and more deterrent to a would-be aggressor, than any force of the 1914 pattern—a mere drop in the bucket of a Continental struggle between mass armies.

This view made headway in Government circles last winter, but in the end the force of past custom prevailed, and the idea of sending a field force was again adopted. Since then, however, there have been fresh developments, both in the international and in the technical sphere, to strengthen doubts of its wisdom. And the fresh strain caused by the Palestine emergency has shown how limited are the resources of the Army for dealing with Continental in addition to colonial problems. That experience has given renewed force to the argument that Britain should limit her Continental commitments to possible action by air and sea. On this question largely turns the trend of her strategic policy, and of still broader issues.

PART II: PROBLEMS

7

The Tactical Problem—and a New Solution

IT IS SETTING EXPECTATIONS HIGH TO COUNT on any programme of rearmament and mechanization to bridge the gulf that now separates armies from their desire—for successful attack. My own view is that these potential developments in offensive power are far exceeded by the actual growth, largely unrecognized, of defensive power: and that the progress of mechanization hitherto has already reinforced the capacity for resistance more than it has any good prospect of strengthening the capacity for attack. Not only fire, but the means of obstruction and of demolition, may now be moved more swiftly to any threatened spot, to thwart a hostile concentration of force.

The question which armies must face is whether they have any chance of overcoming resistance on present lines, even when developed. An alternative way of approaching the problem is to seek a tactical solution, not merely a material one. If we are doubtful of overcoming the defence by an increase of offensive strength, as we have cause to be, is there any prospect in a different solution by an improvement of *art?* So heavy are the present odds against effective action on land, however, that something more than the art of the individual general is needed. Even if an army could breed Napoleons, which no army can be expected to do under its peace-time professional conditions, they would make no headway without an antidote to the paralyzing machine-gun. Armies need to develop a new technique, and, then, to develop their tools to suit this new type of art.

Four years ago a committee composed of the younger generals was appointed to investigate the lessons of the war, and to see whether they were adequately applied in the training of the British Army. The experience then sifted and collated should have shaken satisfaction with customary methods. It is common knowledge that this re-examination of war experience led to the conclusion that surprise was of paramount importance, both in attack and in defence, and that the greatest lesson of the last war was that no attack on an enemy in action was likely to succeed unless his resistance was already paralyzed by surprise in some form. It is known too, that this committee expressed the emphatic opinion that tactical methods, both during and since the war, were too stereotyped; also that the vital importance of surprise and of the indirect approach ought to receive greater attention in the training of the army.

There has been some evidence of efforts, both in Britain and elsewhere, to apply this admonition—but they have not gone wide enough. Exercises have too often become a competition in obviousness. Instead of developing ingenuity, the main effort has too often been towards simplifying the enemy's problem in defending himself. This tendency was the sequel, paradoxically, to the fresh concentration of attention on training for European warfare—the very type of warfare in which investigation had shown the paramount importance of surprise. Under the influence of this "European" key-note methods became more stereotyped rather than more subtle. Instead of going forward to the trial of new ideas, they went back to the repetition of old practices. If this is the best we can hope for, there should be no hesitation in bowing to the present paramountcy of the defensive, and resigning ourselves to the conclusion that it would be better to relegate armies to a merely protective role—as a lesser evil than their futile sacrifice.

There have been, however, some features in the work of the troops, as contrasted with the ruling ideas, which hold out some promise of greater effect. One is the increased skill and subtlety which many of the troops show in concealing themselves from air observation. Another is the cultivation of night sense and increased use of attacks in the dark—by some commanders at least.

These developments point a path by which further progress is possible. By the skilful use of *obscurity*, in its various forms, the attack might recover some of its lost power. Whereas to-day a mass attack merely spells massacre, a "masked attack", under cover of darkness or fog, natural or artificial, has potentialities that have scarcely been tapped. Obscurity is a strong antidote to the defensive machine-gun and may prove a better protection than armour. Its risks are mainly those of confusion; they are certainly less than those of annihilation by machine-

guns with a clear field of fire; and they can be greatly
reduced by training. The superiority of well-trained
troops over normal troops is much more pronounced in
the dark than in daylight.

The use of obscurity, however, requires judicious
adaptation to the type of troops, and a recognition of its
limits. Darkness is a better cloak than artificial fog to
attacking infantry because, if skilled, they can see
through it; when moving in fog the man on foot has
difficulty in keeping his direction, while he becomes a
target the moment he emerges. Thus artificial fog would
seem to have greater promise as a cloak for armoured
fighting vehicles, equipped with direction finders. But
night, despite its advantages for infantry who are trained
in night fighting, has the disadvantage of limiting the
effective depth of their attack. They may storm a position under cover of it, but if they press on, the risks of
confusion are likely to increase disproportionately to the
distance travelled. For control can hardly be kept once
advancing troops are engaged in actual night combat.
The actual assault may go well; the difficulty comes in
re-forming and pushing on afterwards. Perhaps the problem of exploiting the night attack, and extending its
reach, may eventually be solved by some form of flood-
lighting the battlefield when the enemy's position has
been stormed.

In places that afford plentiful cover—woods, villages
and rough ground—infantry may be able to overcome
hostile machine-guns and make headway by the use of
what one may call the "stalking attack". It is a method
which puts a premium on individual skill, and it offers

considerable scope for development. But enthusiasm for it should not blind us to its limitations. It is a method which only fits special conditions; it is bound to be slow if it is to be efficiently executed; and it cannot be counted on to produce large-scale results. It is of its nature a preparatory or supplementary part of the attack rather than a separate form of attack.

We are thus left with the "masked attack" or the "armoured attack" as the two main forms of the offensive that seem to have any promise of breaking into an enemy's position, and ejecting him. But there are more ways of overcoming the enemy's army than by storming its positions, just as there are more ways of winning wars than by winning battles. It is for the art of war to find them, and the need is the greater now that the strength of the defensive has made the storming of positions such a dubious proposition. The enemy may be forestalled on positions; he may be levered out of them by manœuvre; he may be left in them while his general situation is weakened by developing pressure elsewhere, in directions that his position does not cover. As a sequel or otherwise, he may be caught in motion, without having time to take up a defensive disposition.

There may be more scope for such alternative forms of action than is realized by those who still think of another war in terms of the last. The present trend of conditions is by no means favourable to the formation of continuous fronts, at any rate in the early stages of a war. Mass armies do not lend themselves to mechanization, and since the mechanized fractions will be available earlier than the rest, there is a likelihood that the crucial first phase of a war will be fought out between these opposing fractions; thus we should see relatively small forces on large fronts. Furthermore, the assembly of the masses on the frontiers will be hindered by the danger of air attack on the marching columns, and by the jeopardy of supply when their communications are exposed to interruption over so large an area in rear.

A factor common to all these alternative courses is the time factor. If the advantage is to be gained there must be an acceleration of action. The scales of war are inclining not to the side which has the "big battalions" but to the side which "gets there" first. I would suggest that it is an axiom of modern war that "a hundred men with machine-guns who arrive at a spot first are stronger, at least in daylight, than five hundred and sometimes a thousand who arrive second".

This, in turn suggests the value of using any fragment of one's force that is mechanized, or can be motor-moved, to jump ahead and secure key-points. Nothing has been more disappointing in recent years' exercises than the way that mechanization has been wasted by moving units and formations at the pace of their slowest portion, owing to the desire to move complete. It shows a too complete disregard of another modern axiom, arising from the advantage of defence over attack, which we may express in the phrase that "possession is nine-tenths of the war".

Soldiers to-day are predominantly concerned with the problem of attack, so dubious of solution. They might wisely spare a little time to study the possibilities of a form of action which would throw the burden of that problem on the enemy. I refer to what I would term the "baited offensive", the combination of offensive strategy with defensive tactics. Throughout history it has proved one of the most effective of moves, and its advantages have increased as modern weapons have handicapped other types of move. By rapidity of advance and mobility of manœuvre, you may be able to seize points which the enemy, sensitive to the threat, will be constrained to attack. Thus you will invite him to a repulse which in turn may be exploited by a riposte. Such a counter-stroke, against an exhausted attacker, is much less difficult than the attack on a defended position. The opportunity for it may also be created by a calculated withdrawal—what one may call the "luring defensive". Here is another gambit of future warfare.

Whatever form of action be adopted, its effectiveness will depend on concealment of intention. The mystification of the opponent acts upon him like a paralyzing drug. The surest method of producing it, as centuries of experience have shown, is that of *wide extension*. It is a method unsuited for use by military mediocrity. But in skilled hands its risks are far outweighed by its advantages. By operating on a wide front, one thickens the fog of war for one's opponent yet minimizes it for oneself. It is a psychological smoke-screen which disturbs the mind and may shake the nerve of the stoutest adversary. Under cover of it, one has the best chance of seizing points of leverage. The introduction of mechanized mobility has added to its potency while increasing its safety. But of itself it aids rapidity—by reducing the congestion inherent in the practice of operating on narrow fronts.

There have been some instances in recent exercises of a tendency towards movement on wider fronts, but it has not gone nearly far enough for its promise to mature. The greatest hindrance is the dogma of "concentration", imperfectly understood. It is not easy for the simple mind to grasp that concentration is in essence a matter of effect and not of form. The adaptation of methods to changing conditions is retarded by the soldier's customary reluctance to change his traditional terminology. By putting new ideas in old potted terms we cramp the growth of this understanding. I learnt this lesson when compiling the post-war infantry manual. To eradicate the practice of a rigid linear advance and of direct reinforcement—a "building up of the firing line" which merely piled up the casualties—it was necessary to replace the terms "firing line" and "supports" which many, from habit or sentiment, desired to retain. The benefit of their disappearance was unmistakable. But to-day, in a higher sphere, we still suffer such needless handicaps. We still call the preliminary distribution of forces, however widely disposed, the "strategic concentration". We ought to drop this terminological absurdity. Again the idea of advancing on a wide front is cramped by the term "advanced guard", which is associated with the practice of moving on a narrow front—with the whole division on a single road. We are likely to be fettered to this obsolete method until we strike out the term.

The greatest need to-day is to recognize the evolution that is in process. Until the end of the 18th century, a physically concentrated approach, both strategic (*to* the battlefield) and tactical (*on* the battlefield) was the rule. Then Napoleon, exploiting Bourcet's ideas and the new divisional system, introduced a *distributed* strategic approach—the army moving in independent fractions. But the tactical approach was still, in general, a concentrated one. Towards the end of the nineteenth century, with the development of fire weapons, the tactical approach became *dispersed*, i.e. in particles, to diminish the effect of fire. But the strategic approach had again become concentrated—this was due partly to the growth of masses, and partly to the misunderstanding of the Napoleonic method. To-day we must recognize the need of reviving the distributed strategic approach, if there is to be any chance of reviving the art and effect of strategy. But two new conditions—air power and motor power—seem to point to its further development into a *dispersed strategic approach*. The danger of air attack, the aim of mystification, and the need of drawing full value from mechanized mobility, suggest that advancing forces should not only be distributed as widely as is compatible with combined action, but be dispersed as much as is compatible with cohesion. And the development of wireless is a timely aid towards reconciling dispersion with control.

If there is to be any hope of reviving an army's effectiveness, except in mere protectiveness, it lies in the development of such new methods; methods which aim at permeating and dominating areas rather than capturing lines; at the practicable object of paralyzing the enemy's action rather than the theoretical object of crushing his forces. Fluidity of force may succeed where concentration of force merely entails a helpless rigidity. The sea is stronger than a steam-roller, and should replace it as our military ideal. The main difficulty is the doubtful ability of soldiers trained on present lines to rise to the level of this new technique. Unless they can do so, it would be wiser to abandon any dreams of attack, and resign ourselves to the present fact that the defensive is the only role an army can effectively play in a modern war where both sides are fairly equal in equipment.

8

The Capital Ship

THE CAPITAL COST OF THE LAST CAPITAL ships Britain built before the Washington Treaty was some $35,000,000 apiece. Since then constructional costs have risen; whereas that of H.M.S. *Nelson* was $880 for each standard ton, compared with a pre-war battleship cost of $390, the constructional cost of the recent cruisers has been $1020 to the ton compared with $350 in 1914. The cost of new battleships will be at least $40,000,000 each. Beyond that must be reckoned fully two and a half million dollars a year for its direct maintenance, apart from the cost of graving docks and repair plant. Since the building of battleships will absorb so large a proportion of the money that can be found for defence as a whole, it is essential to enquire whether the result promises to repay the cost.

Because of the high valuation which Englishmen have come to place upon sea-power, from centuries of experience, there is a tendency to shirk this question. It would be a happy thing for the British as a people if the conditions of sea-power had not been affected by new developments. For that reason they should be specially on their guard lest the wish should father any unjustified assumption—as it certainly did before the Mediterranean emergency produced an awakening. Is it a full awakening? Has Britain taken the measure of her present sea problems? The question whether aircraft can sink battleships is but a small part of the greater issue whether the battle-fleet can fulfil its strategic role. Under the conditions now developing, has a rebuilt battle-fleet the promise of contributing in a way commensurate with its cost to the security of her sea communications and the flow of supplies upon which the nation's life depends? Is it still the necessary foundation of the operations of the lighter craft which actually execute this task?

In considering these questions we have to take into account the fact that twenty years ago the submarine attack on Britain's shipping routes nearly brought her to disaster despite the unassailable supremacy of her battle-fleet. If she is disposed to forget this, other powers do not. And it would be folly to ignore the fact that they are counting on aircraft and high-speed surface craft to multiply greatly the past potentialities of the submarine for direct attack on sea traffic. We should take account also of the fact that before a new battle-fleet less susceptible to air attack can be built several years must elapse: during that time the means of attack may be improved proportionately. Moreover, a battle-fleet is dependent on bases. The bases that might be developed to-day as safely out of reach may be within easy range of air attack three years hence. The problem is a bundle of complexities. In default of a better answer, the comment is frequently heard that so long as some countries proclaim their intention to build large battleships others must follow suit. This merely shirks the real question. It may also play into the former's hands, by enabling them at some cost to cause a naval power like Britain to divert a much larger proportion of her expenditure into a channel which potential opponents inwardly regard as irrelevant to the vital issue.

In deciding upon its defence programme in 1935, which included the laying down of two new battleships, the British Government was naturally guided by the case presented by the Chiefs of Staff Committee, as then constituted. Of its members, it could hardly be expected that the Chief of the Air Staff should have opposed the claims of the others. And it would be strange if the representatives of the older services, after a lifetime spent in dealing with familiar material, should not hold the shoemaker's belief that "there is nothing like leather". Men rarely reach such a position, especially in peace-time, unless they conform to the accepted ideas. Even in the slow changing past, accepted ideas have commonly proved out of date when tested by war's reality. The likelihood is greater to-day. Since the Services are separate there is no such thing as a professional "Combined Serviceman"—trained in studying war as a whole. The nearest approach to it in Britain is in those who have been through the Imperial Defence College, which has only been established eight years. And it is significant that its first Commandant, Admiral Richmond, has strongly questioned the value of the big battleship under modern conditions. In a letter to *The Times* on December 21st, 1935, he pointed out that the real question is

not whether the battle-fleet may be sunk by air-bombers
but whether it can fulfil its functions—whether, as effective bombing range extends, it will "be able to take up
and maintain a position close enough to its opponent,
either at sea or in harbour, to ensure that that enemy
cannot move without the risk of being brought to action". For if that cannot be done "the fleet becomes
incapable of exercising control". Here is a question that
deserves enquiry. It bears on a point made by the then
First Lord of the Admiralty, Lord Monsell, that "in the
last war our Battle-Fleet in the North Sea was able to
prevent the German Fleet from getting out into the
Atlantic" and "destroying our trade". It is by no means
certain that such a danger was prevented only by the
battle-fleet, but even if it be accepted we have to remember that Britain was greatly favoured by her geographical situation. Would it apply to-day when spaces
are greater, bombing ranges ever increasing, and bases
more distant from an enemy's naval ports?

To meet the doubts which were widely felt and expressed, the British Government in the spring of 1936
belatedly appointed a sub-committee of the Committee
of Imperial Defence to investigate the question of the
vulnerability of capital ships to air attack—a question
which was but a fraction of the issue. The Sub-Committee consisted of four ministers; with the First Sea
Lord (the Chief of the Naval Staff) and the Chief of the
Air Staff as expert advisers. Their report was published
in November 1936. The conclusion is of a cautiously
negative kind, as was to be expected in view of the
limited state of knowledge at the present time on many

of the points at issue, and the natural reluctance to make grave decisions on a basis which is largely speculative. The dominant feeling of the sub-committee is obviously expressed when they dwell on the risks of a false decision, ask whether Britain ought to take the lead in doing away with capital ships, and answer: "Surely not, unless the question is settled beyond all possible doubt." A question which remains, however, is whether it would have been possible to have gained more light on the problem without waiting for the actual experience of war.

In regard to determining the effect of bombs on ships, the sub-committee declare that they are satisfied that the Admiralty "have taken all proper steps to that end", but go on to recommend further experiments, emphasizing that the provision of funds and material should not be allowed to stand in the way. In view of the immense sum of money that is to be sunk in the building of new battleships, surely it should not have been impracticable to have carried out adequate bombing tests on those which have been sent to the scrapheap? Again, on the question of the accuracy of bombing, the sub-committee remarks that some of the factors are "at present a matter of opinion, but we do not think it need so remain. We recommend that experiments, jointly agreed and jointly analyzed, should be carried out to determine the facts." It is clear there was cause here for dissatisfaction. On the effects of anti-aircraft fire, the report refers to "the unreal conditions" under which tests have "hitherto taken place"; it suggests that the difference between the Admiralty's and the Air Ministry's point of view might be "considerably narrowed down by making, as we recommend, peace-time practice assimilate more closely to war conditions". It urges that the two staffs should work in closer touch "for their joint benefits". The impression is left that the eighteen years since the war have not been adequately utilized for objective research. The neglect may be to the joint detriment of the country and the taxpayer.

The many elements of doubt on these technical and tactical issues must have increased the sub-committee's difficulties in studying the broader issues. For they found it necessary to go beyond their terms of reference, since a strict interpretation would have made the field of enquiry artificially narrow. It would, as they justly point out, "be unsatisfactory to deal with the vulnerability of capital ships to air attack without taking account of the extent to which they may become liable to this form of attack". At the same time the sub-committee "tried to confine within necessary limits" their survey of the wider aspects. To determine what are necessary limits, however, must have been difficult. There is no true dividing line between technical, tactical, and strategic values. In historical experience, nothing is more upsetting to calculations than the tendency, natural though it be, to consider the problems of war in bits. At every step the bit needs to be related to the whole. The report bears evidence of the difficulty which this investigation found in endeavouring to keep within limits. It wanders into the field of strategy and out again; the excursion was necessary, but its extent is too short. In concluding it the sub-committee remark: "It is possible to state the matter in its simplest terms. The advocates of the extreme air view would wish this country to build no capital ships (other Powers still continuing to build them). If their theories turn out well-founded, we have wasted money; if ill-founded, we would, in putting them to the test, have lost the Empire."

While there is much truth in this contrast, it is too simple strategically. Britain was in peril of losing the war in 1917, although she had a far larger battle-fleet than to-day, because of the havoc that a comparatively small number of submarines played with her trade routes, and because the destroyers which were wanted to combat that threat were being kept to safeguard the battle-fleet. If Germany had invested in submarine building earlier, some of the money which she devoted to battleships, that menace might well have proved fatal. That is an example of the strategic factors which should be borne in mind when weighing the capital ship question. The sub-committee, while recognizing the risks which the battle-fleet may run in the narrow seas, rightly emphasizes the importance to us of free passage for our trade on the oceans, which "cannot at present be covered by our own land-based air forces". It then remarks that "it would not be impossible for the capital ships of a hypothetical enemy, in the absence of a powerful British fleet, to place themselves, without interference, across our trade routes". Here, certainly, is the strongest argument for the maintenance of capital ships.

Yet it is well to consider the degree of possibility, and to remember the difficulty of "placing" a battle-fleet at a great distance from its bases. For a practical estimate,

too, it is desirable to avoid too vague an hypothesis, and
to ask what Powers there are which possess battleships
that could be used to interrupt any vital section of
Britain's trade routes. Two of them lie at distances which
seem to minimize the possibility of interrupting any vital
route—apart from the fact that only one of these can be
regarded as a possible foe. The others lie in land-locked
areas from which emergence would be very hazardous
to them in face of strong flotilla and air forces. If there
was an outstanding feature of the last war at sea it was
the general reluctance to hazard irreplaceable battleships
in waters where submarines might be lurking, thereby
imposing a marked strategic limitation on the use of battleships. Those hazards are, at the least, multiplied to-day
by the development of aircraft and high-speed motor
torpedo boats, which might be carried on the defender's
ships, and perhaps also of his ocean-going submarines.
Nevertheless, if there is a serious chance of such a venture being attempted and succeeding, Britain may be
justified in building battleships to meet it. Even so, there
are further considerations worth attention.

The navies of to-day are seeking to increase the speed
of their battleships. What if Britain was to find, too late,
that the enemy's battleships, which had reached the
oceans, outpaced hers, and were able to sweep the trade
routes without being brought to battle? Might her people not regret that the money spent on battleships had
not been invested in more aircraft-carriers and flotilla
craft? The whole question of future war is shrouded in
uncertainties, deeper than ever before in history. Because of the risk of enemy battleships placing themselves

on the ocean trade routes, it may be the safe course to build battleships likewise—although the insurance premium would seem high compared with the risk. But it is well to realize that in covering this risk a risk is inevitably being taken in other aspects of the strategic issue, since the total money that can be devoted to defence is not unlimited.

9

The Future of the Mediterranean

IT IS CHARACTERISTIC OF BRITISH POLICY NOT to look far ahead. This habit is carried to a pitch that can only be appreciated by anyone who has enjoyed an inside view of the workings of the machinery of government. It seems to be beyond the understanding of foreigners, especially of the Latin or Teutonic kinds. They find it not only disconcerting but incredible. Hence the undiminished, because perpetually reinforced, currency of the phrase *"perfide Albion"*. If you try to give them a realistic picture of the way that British policy works, they treat the explanation with a politeness that barely conceals their suspicion. To them it is but one more manifestation of the subtlety with which the British pursue their long-range designs. I have often quoted Harold Nicholson's novel, *Public Faces*, as a perfect picture of how the machine works and great issues are apt to be decided. But to a Continental reader, its humorous treatment of the subject seems to convey the idea that it is mere fantasy, instead of, as it really is, proof of the power to see the facts with a true sense of proportion.

The inability of foreign statesmen and diplomats to

comprehend the "immediacy" of British policy leads them into many pitfalls. They misjudge its course by crediting it with a long-term plan; and then stumble again because they fail to realize that underneath its opportunistic surface is not a plan but a principle—or, rather, an instinctive pattern formed by tradition. Sometimes these Continental misjudgments turn out to the benefit of Britain; sometimes otherwise; but they are usually detrimental to Continental plans. And Britain herself has undoubtedly benefited by the elasticity and adaptability which have been preserved by her reluctance to plan ahead. But this tendency, although often an advantage in the sphere of foreign policy, increases the strain on defence policy. Few emergencies have found Britain adequately prepared to meet them. Here is the clue to the familiar saying that in a war she "only wins one battle—the last one."

The military disadvantages of this dislike of looking ahead were forcibly brought home to the British by the situation produced in the Mediterranean in the early autumn of 1935 when Italy launched her Abyssinian campaign in defiance of the League of Nations. As a leading member of the League, Britain was committed to an endeavour to arrest Italy's course. It placed her in a predicament which few had foreseen. The post-war friction between France and Italy, followed by the growth of Fascist Italy's armed power, had focused attention on the conflict of interests between the two Latin powers. In this, Britain saw the need of her services as mediator, and likewise recognized the divergent possibilities of a clash between Italian and German interests in Austria. She took little account of possible trouble between herself and Italy; Italian propaganda in Malta was an irritation, but seemed a local symptom that could hardly develop in view of the long-standing tradition of friendship between the two countries and Italy's dependence on imported raw materials, together with her obvious susceptibility to the pressure of sea-power. These old-established assumptions helped to obscure the newly roughened edges of Britain's own position in the Mediterranean. Her repose was abruptly disturbed in 1935. When the reality of the Italian threat to Abyssinia was at last appreciated it produced a rise of popular indignation almost comparable to that caused by the violation of "little Belgium"; and the effect, in pushing the Government forward, was accentuated by the backsliding of the Laval Government in France. Forced to give a lead at Geneva in upholding the Covenant, the British found themselves thrust still more into the foreground by their strategic position astride Italy's sea route to East Africa. This made them the natural target if sanctions were to culminate in war. Italy emphasized the point by despatching mechanized divisions and powerful bombing squadrons to her Libyan colony, close to the borders of Egypt. Britain hastily strengthened her forces there, though it meant a temporary interruption of her Air Force expansion at home and stripping the Army of most of its still meagre supply of modern equipment. More precarious still was the position of her main fleet base at Malta which lay within easy range of the Italian air bases; to keep the fleet there, liable to a surprise onslaught by bombers or to lurking submarines was a risk that made the Admiralty hurriedly swallow the vocal disdain of these oversea and undersea weapons in which they had been but recently indulging; the fleet was withdrawn from Malta to the far end of the Mediterranean. Here, certainly, it might block the passage of Italian transports, if the League issue was pressed thus far, but how far it could keep a free passage for Britain's own sea traffic was a question that left the British public wondering.

Some twelve years ago, in a little book on *The Future of War*, I suggested that the controversies over the bomb versus the battleship, or the torpedo versus the gun, tended to overlook the end in their ardour over the means—and that, instead of becoming entangled in an interminable dispute over technical values we ought to "direct our course by the compass of grand strategy". While the power of the fleet might still be paramount on the oceans, it was clear that it had been strategically affected in the narrow seas by the newer weapons. "The vital question of the future is how this transfer of power over the narrow seas affects the international situation— particularly that of Great Britain, which is concerned with both spheres of sea-power." After studying its bearing on the seas around the British Isles I passed on to "the Mediterranean, another long and narrow sea channel through which runs our artery with the East, and where our main naval force is now concentrated. Note that our ships, naval or mercantile, must traverse the *length* of this channel, and worse still, have to filter through a tiny hole at each end—the straits of Gibraltar and the Suez Canal—while midway there is a narrow 'waist' between Sicily and Tunis barely ninety miles across." After pointing out how the potential *radii* of submarine attack from the ports on the European and African coasts intersected this long single line of British sea communications, the question was posed: "Is it not obvious that if in a future war any Mediterranean power was numbered among Britain's enemies, her fleet would find it difficult enough to protect itself against submarines, let alone protect merchant convoys and troop transports? When to the proved menace of submarine power is added the potential effect of aircraft attack against shipping in the narrow seas, it is time the British people awoke to the fact that, in case of such a war, the Mediterranean would be impassable, and that this important artery would have to be abandoned. Thus, as a strategical asset, the Suez Canal has lost a large part of its value in face of modern naval and air development—for in such a war we should be driven to close the Mediterranean route, and divert our imperial communications round the Cape of Good Hope."

It is worth quoting this, not to prove that the writer was wise before the event, but because of its continued bearing on a problem that is not yet solved and on events that may be still to come. I was by no means the only critic who drew attention to the new dangers in the years that have intervened. Yet when the Italian crisis arose, not only was the main British fleet still stationed at Malta, but practically nothing had been done to prepare a "switch" route round the Cape for our sea-traffic. Under pressure of the emergency, part of the traffic from the East which normally passes through the Suez

Canal was actually diverted round the Cape, and hurried steps were taken to send out reserves to the bases along that route. But it became clear that bunkering and port facilities would have to be considerably enlarged if the whole of the traffic was to be sent that way. Also that the naval bases would have to be renovated and developed.

The mentality which had been responsible for the neglect of such obvious precautionary needs can perhaps be best epitomized by an extract from a letter which I received in August, 1935, from one of the highest officers of the Empire: "You have evidently been crammed up, as I fear that both the Government and the public at home have, by the Air propaganda. . . . There is only one way in which the Air can win a war and that is by bombing women and children; and that will never bring a great nation to its knees, but only inferior people. You know perfectly well that the Navy laughs at the Air now. They have got protected decks, and with their 'blisters' and multiple machine-guns and multiple anti-aircraft guns, they don't fear them in the slightest."

Close on the heels of this letter the Fleet abandoned Malta—for fear of what it hadn't feared. The letter is significant not merely as an example of the obscurantism induced by the military prejudices against novelties; it shows how the very men who are concerned with the bigger problems of defence are apt, through their training, to focus their attention on mere tactical details, so that they can overlook the fact that the security of a fleet depends on the security of its bases, not merely on its guns and armour. Also, the bigger fact still, that the purpose of a fleet is not merely its self-preservation, but to preserve the security of the sea-routes.

It is questionable whether these facts have been fully impressed even by the alarm of that autumn. Since then, Britain has exerted herself to remodel as well as strengthen her naval dispositions in the Mediterranean. Thereby she will be in a better position to deal with any recurrence of an Italian threat to her fleet. But it is not easy to see how any reliance can be placed on the use of the Mediterranean route for her own sea-traffic, if such a conflict should arise.

Britain's Mediterranean problem has two main aspects. First, that of ensuring the safe flow of the traffic from the East which uses this short cut. Second, that of maintaining her sphere of influence in the Eastern Mediterranean, and the forces which safeguard her position there. There is a tendency to regard the second as a corollary of the first, but historically the order of development was the reverse. This fact should be borne in mind when considering the treatment of the problem under the new conditions of to-day. Britain's concern with the Eastern Mediterranean was forcibly demonstrated throughout the first half of the nineteenth century, not only in the struggle against Napoleon; but it was not until late in the second half of the century that it became of paramount importance to her sea-communications with India and the East. The Suez Canal was the child of a Frenchman's imagination; and Ferdinand de Lesseps's scheme was stoutly resisted by Lord Palmerston who, seeing it merely as a French attempt to repeat Napoleon's design of conquering Egypt, instructed his diplomatic agents throughout Europe to do all they could to prevent the construction of the canal. In the end the British Government remained the solitary opponent—and failed.

Few failures have been more richly compensated. For this shortening of the route to the East resulted in a ten-fold increase of Britain's trade with the East. It also went a long way towards securing her military position there —by accelerating her power of reinforcing her garrisons. The Canal, begun in 1859, was opened ten years later. And within five years, Britain became the chief share-holder through the foresight of her un-British Prime Minister, Disraeli, in purchasing from the Khedive seven-sixteenths of the total share issue, at a price of £4,000,-000. This stroke of Imperial policy was extended in 1882 by the occupation of Egypt, following the intervention of Britain to suppress Arabi's anti-foreign rising The occupation, intended to be temporary, became perma-nent in the process of reforming the administration. It brought great compensations, but also a chain of com-plications. It assured the security of the Canal, that hun-dred-mile pipe through which now passed Britain's main line of communication with the East, but it imposed a great and growing burden in protecting both the Canal itself and the rest of the homeward route, since, unlike the Cape route, this passed through a sea bordered by other naval powers. Henceforth the British had to main-tain a considerable proportion of their naval strength permanently in the Mediterranean as custodians of the route.

The strain became severe under the indirect pressure

of Germany's naval expansion in the decade before 1914. The growth of their fleet in the North Sea faced the British with a difficult choice between weakness in one quarter and vast expenditure to maintain predominance in both. They found a compromise in an understanding with France whereby they concentrated their strength in home waters and France concentrated hers in the Mediterranean. This proved a tie greater than they had realized in the crisis of 1914, since, with the first threat of war between Germany and France, they found themselves morally committed to the duty of safeguarding the northern coast of France against the German Navy. And in the war the dangers of the Mediterranean route were demonstrated by the high percentage of commerce destruction that was achieved there in proportion to the small force employed by the attacker—there were rarely more than half a dozen submarines operating at any one time. One U-boat alone attained a total "bag" of half a million tons of shipping. A German naval historian records that "U-boat commanders going into the Mediterranean were much envied by their comrades in home waters owing to the extraordinary possibilities offered by operations in the Mediterranean". Yet this campaign was carried on at an immense distance from their home bases and under the great difficulties caused by the hazardous passage past the British Isles and the lack of convenient bases in the Mediterranean.

After the war, with the collapse of Germany's naval power, the British Navy returned in strength to the Mediterranean, and its main fleet was based at Malta. On the surface it seemed to re-establish the old security of the route to India, and although the continued attention given by the French and Italians to submarine construction caused some uneasiness, the ultimate conquest of the U-boats in 1918 tended to make British naval opinion forget the extreme handicaps under which the U-boat campaign had worked, so that the confidence bred of success in the final issue caused an undue discount of the future prospects of the submarine when employed under more favourable conditions. Such conditions are certainly offered to a guerilla campaign in the Mediterranean waged by a naval power which is there in home waters.

It is the advent of air power, however, which has most affected the Mediterranean situation. Its influence did not develop early after the war, although its shadow began to stretch across the inland sea. Italy had no serious air force until Mussolini rebuilt it. Spain has never had one. France herself was too remote from the traffic-route, and although her African colonies bordered it, they were separated by a wide expanse of sea from their sources of aircraft supply. Even if a war between Britain and France had been politically conceivable, the British fleet and its aircraft carriers might have had a powerful effect on the strategic situation of the French by interrupting the passage of trade and reinforcements between France and French North Africa. Moreover, the scope of shore-based air attack was limited by the comparatively short radius of the machines possessed by the post-war air forces.

The situation has radically changed with the rise of Italian air power, the development of bombers that have a radius of 400 to 500 miles, and the promised attainment within a year or two of double this radius. Thereby the 100-mile canal from Suez to Port Said has been extended into a 2000-mile "canal" from Port Said to Gibraltar. Port Said itself lies less than 400 miles from the Italian air bases in the Dodecanese, off the south-west corner of Asia Minor. While limited at present, they are being developed. On emerging from the Port Said bottle-neck, shipping might have a short run of sea-space with only the lesser fear of being caught in the open. But the route then passes through the mere 200-mile channel between Crete and Libya, dominated by the Italian air-base at Tobruk. An alternative route is round the north coast of Crete, but this passes within a bare 100 miles of the Dodecanese islands. Beyond Crete the routes inevitably converge on Malta, a mere 70 miles from the coast of Sicily and less than 200 from Tripoli. Thereafter the channel narrows until it is less than 90 miles across between Sicily and the African coast at Cape Bon. Before any shipping could emerge from this danger zone it would be in a fresh one, created by the Italian air bases in Sardinia, which lies within 100 miles of the African coast. Thus for more than half the length of the Mediterranean shipping passes within easy bombing range of Italian air bases, and for fully three quarters might run the risk of attack. The danger will soon grow as the new types of bomber recently designed, and in process of accelerated production, come into general use.

But a new danger has loomed up, even earlier, to menace the one free stretch of the route—and the bottle-neck at the far end. This is the possibility of a militaristic

Spain, filled with the desire to renew its Imperial role which is already reflected in some of the interviews given by General Franco, and linked with Fascist Italy by a common ambition as well as by the sense of help received in the course of the present rising. In that quarter, too, Nazi Germany might find scope for developing an indirect leverage on her own neighbours in favour of her ambitions. A powerful Spanish Air Force, supplied or constructed by foreign aid, could be a serious menace to the last lap of the Mediterranean route. And Gibraltar in turn might become as untenable as a base for the British fleet as Malta proved in the last emergency. Strategically, the danger is so obvious that it is difficult to understand the eagerness with which some of the most avowedly patriotic sections of the British public have desired the rebels' success. Class-sentiment and property-sense would seem to have blinded their strategic sight. The danger would be extended by the establishment of air and submarine bases in the Balearic Isles; and extended still further, by the similar use of the Canary Isles —since this would threaten Britain's use of the Cape route. There have been reports, formally denied, of a secret promise of these two strategic points to Italy and Germany respectively in return for help rendered. Though the denial may be accepted, this does not remove the potential danger. The availability of bases in these islands for the possible use of a strong sea and air power would be scarcely less ominous than the actual cession of the territory.

The prospect deepens the dark hue of the Mediterranean's new complexion. It jeopardizes the outlook for

France as well as for Britain. France hitherto had, on the whole, more scope for exerting pressure on Italy than the other way round. Her dependence on imported raw materials, and thus on sea communications, was less than Italy's; unlike Italy, she had ports outside the Mediterranean; her sea-traffic from Africa could diminish the chance of interference by hugging the Spanish shore; it might even be possible to avoid the sea passage by using the Spanish railways. Moreover, Italy's industrial centres, lying close to the northern frontier, would be more endangered by air attack than those of France. A Spain in league with Italy, and developed into a formidable military power, would change the balance heavily to the disadvantage of France—who may find increasing cause to regret the tacit encouragement she gave to Italy's successful defiance of the League over Abyssinia and the consequent enhancement of Italy's military prestige.

But the potential effect on Britain's position strategically stretches further. The Spanish development can hardly fail to have an influence on the steps that have been taken to reorganize the British dispositions in the Mediterranean. When the tension arose over Abyssinia last autumn, the main part of the British fleet was withdrawn from Malta to Alexandria. But this has defects as a permanent base, apart from being in Egyptian territory. Also it lies within bombing range of the Italian airbases in Libya and the Dodecanese—some 350 miles from the former and 400 from the latter. These considerations have prompted a study of other possible bases. Cyprus is one. Disraeli secured possession of it at the Berlin Congress of 1878 and presented it to Queen Victoria with the remark: "Cyprus is the key of Western Asia". But four years later its value was eclipsed by the occupation of Egypt, and ever since Cyprus has lain in strategic neglect. After the war, however, the harbour of Famagusta, on the south coast, was improved and enlarged, while in 1931 Imperial Airways temporarily made Limassol a stopping place on their Middle East service. The salt lake near here is suitable for flying boats while the great central plain forms a natural air-base. Another possibility is Haifa, the Palestinian terminus of the oil pipe-line from Iraq. Haifa is at present the most secure from air attack, lying some 660 miles from the nearest air-base in Libya, and 450 from the Dodecanese. But with the rapidly increasing range of aircraft even the most remote base would be brought within bombing range before its development and fortification could be completed, while the farther away that the fleet and its own aircraft carriers are posted the more its own power of action against an enemy is handicapped.

Confronted with this dilemma, the present inclination of the British Admiralty would seem to be "to damn the risks" and trust in the superiority of its own offensive power. Preparations along these lines are foreshadowed by the recent statement of the First Lord of the Admiralty on returning from a tour of inspection in the Mediterranean. He declared that there was no intention of "abdicating our position in that sea, or of scuttling from Malta", and added: "It is simply a question of adapting ourselves to the new conditions, and of making the fullest use of our own air power". The question may not be so simple to answer, satisfactorily, when all the conditions are appreciated, but the determination is clear. Malta is to remain the primary base of the British Fleet, and its defences are being strengthened, while the potentialities of Cyprus as an air and naval base are being developed. Cyprus lies 270 miles distant from the new bases which Italy has made in the Dodecanese, and since it offers accommodation for a larger force, while the British also have a superiority in sea-borne aircraft, there is a prospect of converting any threat from the Dodecanese into a boomerang. With superior naval and air force, too, the islands of the Dodecanese might be effectively isolated from support and supply from Italy. So might Libya, while the Italian colonies, old and new, in East Africa are largely dependent on the goodwill of the power which holds the gateway from the Mediterranean into the Red Sea. These aspects of the situation are worth recognition.

Likewise in the western half of the Mediterranean, the new danger to which the French communications with North Africa are exposed does not lessen the inherent weaknesses of Italy, due to her immense length of coastline, the accessibility and vulnerability of her focal points, and her greater need of sea-borne supplies. If she strikes she can hurt, but she runs even more risk of getting hurt. Besides the formidable naval and air power of France, there is the pressure which the British naval forces might be able to exert if they are used with good judgment, and avoid being trapped in harbour. With so great a length of coastline, the protective screen afforded by submarines and shore-based aircraft might not prove impenetrable, while the strain on Italy's armed resources is increased by the number of her detached territories. The British Mediterranean Fleet has already been strengthened and a large proportion of the new ships now under construction at home are likely to be sent to reinforce it further.

It is a bold bid which Britain is thus making to maintain her threatened position in the Mediterranean by establishing a more formidable deterrent to interference. Inevitably it has some element of a gamble, because of the uncertainty which veils so many of the technical issues of modern warfare. But its chances will certainly be increased or decreased according to the "load" that her forces carry. If they are called on to maintain the use of the Mediterranean as a mercantile traffic-route from the East the odds will be heavily against the attempt succeeding, while the effort will dissipate and endanger their own strength. If the British Admiralty is prepared to abandon this route and divert all normal traffic by the Cape route, its forces in the Mediterranean may play an important strategic part. The diversion increases the distance from Bombay to England by nearly eighty per cent—from 5900 miles to 10,400 miles; from Singapore by over forty per cent—from 7900 miles to 11,400 miles; but from Melbourne, only ten per cent—from 10,700 miles to 11,800 miles. The increased distance would cause delay, and a consequent check in the flow of supplies unless and until more shipping was employed on the route. But even a delay would not have very serious effects on Britain's supply situation. For only twenty per cent of her imports at present come through the Mediterranean. And of these eleven per cent come from countries within that sea, so that a readjustment in the scheme of supply regarding these commodities would in any case be inevitable to meet the conditions of war. But the use of the Cape route for the remainder of the Eastern trade would simplify the strategic problem of the British in a war with any Mediterranean power. By the virtual closing of that sea as a traffic-route it might be more effectively utilized as an area of offensive operations against an opponent who could not disencumber himself similarly.

A people who are anxious for peace and a quiet life are naturally inclined to look at a strategic problem from the point of view of their own security, and thus to overlook the disabilities of a potential opponent. The way that Italy has enlarged her forces and extended her bases of offensive action has undoubtedly complicated Britain's problem in assuring the security of her trade-routes and overseas territories. But in the process of extending, Italy has entangled her bases with those of Britain to an extent that is awkward for herself. This strategic entanglement may prove a check on aggression, and thereby become an unforeseen "bond" of peace.

A new disturbing factor has been foreshadowed by the possibility of Spain's development into a military power with warlike tastes and Fascist ties. This would be a potential threat not only to the French communications with her African colonies, but to Britain's power to control the western outlet from the Mediterranean. A naval force could hardly be maintained at Gibraltar in face of a hostile air force on the mainland.

These possibilities inevitably increase the insecurity of

the British position in the Mediterranean, while they also introduce a new insecurity into the Cape route. Even so, the fresh complications might not prove wholly adverse. When so many heavily armed powers are confined in so narrow a space, each with their bases interwoven, and that space is being continuously narrowed by the growth of modern weapons, to start a war there would be like shutting up a bunch of mad cats in a cage. The picture, and the uncertainty of any calculations, might deter even the most warlike statesman.

10

The Role of the British Army

THERE IS A TENDENCY IN ALL COUNTRIES FOR the people to congratulate themselves on the security they will gain by their present programmes of rearmament. The notion was carried furthest by the recent assertion of Herr Rudolf Hess: "Every new gun, every new tank, every aeroplane, gives an additional security to the German mother that her children will not be slaughtered in an accursed war." A more realistic view would tell us that any country's situation is, and is likely to be, far less secure than it was before the new armament race began. And it is all too likely that the completion of a programme will be more than a stage in an extending programme. Nevertheless, there is no security in remaining weak when surrounded by those who believe that virtue rests with the violent. Arming becomes unavoidable for those who are unwilling to be victims. The question is, then, how to arm to the best effect proportionately to the expense. It requires not only a clear idea of the aim but a sure gauge of the resources and their relative values.

In such a trial of strength a nation's capacity to stand

the strain depends not merely on the extent of its resources but on their economic distribution. That lesson is engraved in Britain's history. Where Spain, Holland, and France broke down in turn under the double strain of spreading their military effort in the attempt to bestride both the land and the sea, she conserved her strength, helped by geography, by concentrating on superiority in one element. To-day the two elements have become three by the addition of the air, which brings the consequent risk of a triple strain. It lies with her defence policy to minimize this, by maintaining a sense of proportion. Security in the air is as necessary to her as security on the seas; she cannot safely concentrate on one at the expense of the other, although by wise distribution and combination she may be able to diminish the total burden thus created. Moreover, in each case there are standards by which she can gauge her needs; it is true that if she stands alone these represent an appalling effort and expense, but they can be scaled down on the basis of collective security, in proportion as such a basis can be established.

In the sphere of the land forces·Britain is, fortunately, free of any standards imposed by the strength of the Continental armies. The only essential requirement is to maintain forces sufficient to defend, and maintain order in, her overseas territories. For those forces a mobile Imperial reserve is needed. Anything beyond this is not a strategic obligation, although it may be prompted by political considerations. The use of a field force to prevent hostile air and submarine bases being established close to her own coast may be desirable strategically, but is not strictly essential. Its value must be weighed against its cost—lest it be at the expense of the necessities—and against its risks both political and military. Its practicability should also receive due attention—can' it be provided without detriment to the essential function of the army? Can it be sufficiently effective under the modern conditions of war, and the limitations imposed by geography? To answer such questions we must try to estimate those conditions and the fitness of the British Army to meet them.

The experience of the last war left the defensive still superior to the offensive in land warfare. For it would be rash to draw different conclusions from the last phase when morale was crumbling and resources were becoming exhausted. Thus anticipations of a change are merely built on hope—the hope that the subsequent development of certain of the new weapons of the last war may suffice to overcome the power of defence, even though this has also been developed. Military history is such a tale of misplaced hopes that we need to examine such assumptions with care before building a defence policy upon them.

The one factor which is clear is that an expeditionary force, should Britain use one, will need the power of attack in order to fulfil its purpose under the conditions that can be foreseen. For, if it is to be sent complete with all its arms and transport, it cannot be transhipped to the Continent and brought into action until some time has elapsed—in 1914 this was three weeks, and although accelerated mobilization arrangements may reduce it to some extent there is the question whether the modern risk of air attack will allow it to be moved by as direct a route as in 1914. By the time it arrives, the war, owing to the accelerated tempo of modern plans, is likely to have taken a definite turn. The aggressor may have been stopped on the frontier; in this case the expeditionary force might have no purpose except to be used in an offensive against his frontier. The aggressor may have penetrated some distance and then have been stopped; in this case the force would be called on to help in ejecting him by an offensive. The aggressor may be still pressing on—even in this case, the counter-offensive is the most likely form of action it would be called on to undertake. All these prospects imply that an expeditionary force, if it is to be sent, should possess the power of attack. Is there any adequate prospect of its possessing this power?

Before attempting an answer, it is worth while examining the basic elements of the tactical problem that the force would have to solve if it gets to grips with the enemy without its strategic advance being interrupted by air attack.

The predominant condition of the last war, on land, was the superiority of the defensive. During four years this superiority amounted to supremacy. The main cause was the machine-gun. In the spring of 1918 the Germans were able temporarily to overcome the Allied defence, partly through the aid of a new technique, but even more through the unforeseen help of fog, which blanketed the opposing machine-guns at the outset of their first three offensives. Later, when there was no fog, their offensives failed. And even their successful offensives petered out in face of slender opposition when this was reinforced by their own difficulties in maintaining momentum. In the late summer and autumn of 1918 the German defence in turn was overcome by the combination of tanks with natural and artificial fog. Even so, the Allies never succeeded in solving the problem of exploiting initial success, not even as far as the Germans had done. The cause of their greater, and conclusive, success lay in the moral and physical bankruptcy of the foe, whose military ruin could be traced to the expense of his own spectacular offensives earlier, and was completed by the sickness, physical and mental, of his troops which was produced by economic pressure. The coming of the Germans' collapse found the Allied armies baffled, at least for the time, by the problem of keeping up armed pressure.

Analysis of these conditions provides no warrant for the belief that the offensive, save locally, had succeeded in reducing the superiority of the defensive. They rule out the idea that infantry who have to attack over the open can, even locally, be expected to overcome infantry whose machine-guns are ensconced behind cover, so long as the defending side is morally unshaken. The new light machine-guns are certainly an improvement on the cumbersome types of the past, for use by advancing troops, but there is no ground for supposing that they are going to make a decisive difference against an enemy who is below ground. High-angle fire, since it drops the projectiles over the cover, is more promising; but we cannot expect a decisive difference to be made by the infantry mortars, against fifty or sixty machine-guns on an opposing battalion front. There were mortars in the last war.

The possible scale of artillery support is a trifle compared with what it was in the offensives of the last war, and we know how little it achieved then. By contrast, any defending force in Western Europe to-day will have far more machine-guns to check the attack than it had then. Moreover, if motorization has quickened the application of fire-power in the attack, it promises to help the defence even more by enabling him to rush machine-guns to any threatened spot and counteract any surprise that the attacker achieves. The defending machine-guns will be able to fire from behind cover, whereas the attackers, at any rate in the immediate future, will have to be brought forward in unshielded vehicles. They might make more difference if they were mounted in armoured vehicles and could bring their fire forward to close ranges.

What further possibilities are there of overcoming the established superiority of the defence? Leaving gas out of the reckoning, we have to pin our hopes of a solution to *obscurity*, *armour*, and *art*. Attacking infantry have at present a good chance of overcoming the machine-gun in the dark, although art and high training are required to profit by the opportunity and avoid the risks of confusion. Even so, they cannot safely press the attack more than a short distance; to exploit the effect there must be enough armoured vehicles available, or some form of flood-lighting the battlefield must be invented. Also, it would be unwise to bank too heavily on

the attack in darkness, for the defence may find means
of keeping their front continuously lighted.

The attack in fog has perhaps greater possibilities, on
the basis of experience; but we cannot count on enjoying
a natural fog when we need it. Smoke-screens are a useful substitute, but those of the past were too local. More
hope lies in the development of artificial fog, capable of
being projected in larger volume than is possible with
artillery smoke-shell. Even so, the defence may not be
long in finding means of dispersing it.

Armour is another well-proved aid. The armour may
be carried, as in the war, by relatively slow tanks accompanying the infantry. It may be carried by fast tanks
acting like cavalry in earlier wars and relying on the
speed of the charge or on rapidity of manœuvre. It may
be carried, also, by little low-built machines manned by
infantry, relying partly on their slight visibility, and
giving the infantryman more protection at least than he
would have when advancing on foot—the possibilities of
such true "mechanized infantry" have not yet been fully
explored. The value of armour can also be increased by
combining it with the use of obscurity. Armoured
troops, if equipped with direction-finders, may be more
suited to profit by natural or artificial fog than are men
on their feet. In darkness, too, they are more formidable,
if adequately trained for such tactics. And the progress
that may be made in dispersing obscurity on behalf of
the defence should affect tanks less because of their
speed, so long as some obscurity remains.

Nevertheless, the post-war development of anti-tank
weapons is a serious and increasing threat to the tank,

especially when coupled with the new technique of obstruction. How serious, it is not easy to gauge. We can at
least be clear that the chances of the tanks increase with
their quantity—and decrease disproportionately when
they are few. At present the British Army contemplates
no more than its one existing tank brigade re-equipped
with modern machines—which may form part of a mobile division otherwise possessing small power of attack
—and four battalions of infantry tanks which have still
to be built. With such a small quantity of tanks, the
chances of successful attack might well be zero. Against
the multiplying anti-tank weapons of to-day, it is certain that hope lies only in swarms—to swamp the defence.

For the rest of the army, the ordinary infantry divisions, there is just a possibility that the development of a
new technique in combination with the new equipment
might give them some prospect of successful attack, up
to a point. This possibility depends on progress in the
art of war rather than on its material side. Here, un-
fortunately, we have to face the fact that the Army's
present lack of modern equipment is not the sum of its
qualitative deficiencies. Because of their small size the
British forces need to excel in technical and tactical skill.
At present they do not. Hampered by the poor type of
recruits it has attracted, by the depressingly slow promotion among the officers, by the peace-time tendency to
give staff work preference over leadership, by the lack
of men and new means with which to develop the art
of command, and by years of an atmosphere in which
boldness of thought and freedom of expression were dis-

couraged, the Army as a whole is not up to the standard
of skill demanded by the more exacting conditions of
modern warfare. It may be no worse than other armies,
but it does not stand out like the army of 1914, while
the true standard required is relative to the conditions
of warfare, not merely to the level of others. Its weaknesses are apparent not merely to the onlooker, who is
said proverbially to see most of the game; they are realized by many of the officers concerned with its training.
It will be easier to make good the material deficiencies
than to remedy these failings. The energy now being
exerted may complete the re-equipment of the Army
within two or three years. Even under the best guidance,
and a better sense of how to promote activity of intelligence, it would take many years to outgrow the legacy
of the post-war period and raise the general level of tactical aptitude. There are a fair number of officers who
are real tacticians, whose natural aptitude has survived
an unfavourable climate, but the proportion to the total
is too small. They are like currants in a pudding.

There has been an unpalatable abundance of suet in
the exercises seen in recent years. "Safety first," seems
to have largely superseded Danton's, and Napoleon's,
motto *"l'audace, l'audace, toujours l'audace"*. Conform-
ity to the manuals, the confusion due to constant changes
of detail, and the excessive emphasis on meticulous order-
writing, have produced a slow-motion habit which is
inimical to the exploitation of opportunities. Instead of
building tactical art on a basis of battle-drill, thus quick-
ening its application, we have turned tactics into a drill
in slow time. The effect is seen in an attitude of what

can only be described as "reckless caution". It is the opposite of real security, while it stultifies the possibility of achieving surprise. To-day we are slaves of the obvious instead of being masters of surprise. Without a far more highly developed battle-craft there can be but a dim prospect of shaking the sovereignty of the defence.

When all the conditions are carefully weighed, the balance seems to be heavily against the hope that a British field force on the Continent might have a military effect commensurate with the expense and the risk. I cannot see an adequate prospect, even when the present programme is complete, of its possessing the power of attack necessary to wrest from an invader any ground he may have gained before it could arrive. To fit the picture into the actual frame, formed by the zone between the Meuse and the Channel, serves to deepen this impression. And I do not see that a larger force would have a better effect, nor that subsequent reinforcement might make a great difference, for the limiting conditions have little to do with numbers of men. They are essentially qualitative and technical. Moreover, beyond all the difficulties which face the attacker on land lies the danger of his approach being dislocated by hostile attack from the air. And the larger the force the greater the danger.

It may still be considered that the force is worth while on political grounds. That may be a just opinion. But those who decide ought to do so with their eyes opened to the fundamental military limitations. Moreover, the latest turn of Belgian policy may well give pause to those who are inclined to assume the need of a field force for the Continent without being clear as to the way it will act and the end it will serve. It has been argued that the action of the field force should be directed to prevent an enemy's establishing air bases close to England's coast, and to cover the bases which the Air Force might establish abroad in order to lengthen its range. But the increasing range of aircraft promises to diminish the value of such cover. Apart from this doubt of its need, the type of force required for the particular duty is different to that of 1914, when the plans of the General Staff were dominated by the idea of contributing a general-purpose force of three army corps to join the French field armies in their main offensive campaign. Even if a general offensive of this kind were practicable to-day, the distant and disconnected cover it would give might not suffice to protect the air bases under modern strategic conditions. For that function a specially designed force might be more effective, and less precarious. Its design is indicated by the prevailing conditions and limitations of land warfare—a force small in numbers of men but amply equipped with fire-weapons of the light and handy kind, and coupling this power of resistance with high strategic mobility. Its action, too, should be adjusted to these conditions, making the most of the inherent advantages of modern fire-defence, and applying tactics of elastic resistance and riposte.

If, now, there is a doubt as to Belgium's attitude, the difficulties of using a field army effectively may be augmented, and its risks also. If, on the other hand, Britain should decide to give up the idea of intervention with an army, her military problems would be greatly simplified. She could concentrate on making the Army at home an adequate Imperial Reserve, for the reinforcement of the overseas garrisons, the mobile defence of the overseas territories, and for such expeditions, truly so-called, as may be needed to fulfil her historic strategy under future conditions. This would avoid the wide, and increasing, divergence between what is required for offensive warfare on the Continent and what is best suited to mobile defence, to Colonial warfare, and Imperial policing. The forces Britain has would need far less development. Since Marlborough the British Army has rarely shone in the offensive, not through want of courage, but from lack of aptitude. It has been superb in defence, and unrivalled as an agent in maintaining order. Those qualities will have enhanced value in proportion as strategic mobility is added.

Wherever the Army is used, and whatever decision may be taken as to sending a force across the Channel, its mission and action ought to be adjusted to tactical realities. It should not be allowed to waste its strength by becoming engaged in an allied offensive carried out on past and present Continental lines. This does not mean that its action would, or could, always be confined to pure defence. But where a strategic advance was necessary to fulfil its mission, it should normally combine this with tactics of elastic resistance, varied by a lightning riposte to exploit a disordered recoil on the enemy's part, and by dislocating counter-moves. It is folly, nowadays, to attempt direct attack on a properly equipped foe, except at points where the opposition is particularly weak. Even in the past ages of warfare, it has been rare for a strategic offensive to be crowned by a successful attack; modern conditions have emphasized still more the superior promise of the luring defensive or the combination of offensive strategy with defensive tactics. Yet at present, as in the past, the training of armies is predominantly devoted to practising tactics which are essentially unreal, under the spell of a soldierly dream of attack which can only end in nightmare assaults.

II

The adequacy of the Army depends on the question of its functions. When introducing the Army Estimates in 1935, the spokesman of the War Office classified these as—the defence of the home country, the defence of the naval bases, the maintenance of order in the territories of the Empire and the defence of British interests abroad —the last being the function of what was called an "expeditionary force" and is now called a "field force". He went on to say that these four purposes were "all equally important", a statement which might obscure the problem of proportion. For any defence policy in peace, like strategy in war, must necessarily be a reconciliation between conflicting claims. To be equally strong everywhere, against an opponent with equal resources or a superior sense of proportion, entails being too weak everywhere. The impossibility of covering everything is the rock upon which many national policies have foundered. There is a need to classify the purposes in order of importance, and then to see how far the organization that best serves the major purpose can also serve the others.

Changing conditions affect all four purposes. Although the fear of invasion held a considerable proportion of the troops in England during the last war, the fear had no justification in anything that is known of the enemy's intentions, nor in the actual conditions: and now, with the development of air power, these conditions have made such an attempt still more improbable. The approach of a fleet of transports to, and the disembarkation of troops on, a hostile coast have become far more hazardous in face of a shore-based air force. Conditions, therefore, would seem to have diminished the importance of the defence of the home country as a function of the Army, although the Army may well be called on to maintain order and restore internal communications in the dislocation caused by a hostile air attack. Actual defence from the ground against an air attack is a new duty, but one of a specialized kind.

The defence of naval bases is a duty for which only a small fraction of the army is needed. In fulfilling it, troops have always been subsidiary to the naval forces themselves, and may now be considered subsidiary to the defence by air also; if these are worsted, the situation of the military garrison would be more precarious than ever in the past.

More important, certainly, is the Army's duty of policing the overseas territories. In keeping quiet uncivilized or thinly populated territories, and also in checking invasion of frontiers, especially the more remote, air power may play a primary part. But for maintaining order in thickly populated lands nothing is likely, so far as we can foresee, to replace the need for troops on the ground. If the Empire is to be maintained, and unless special policing forces are to be created, this duty must take precedence in the Army's functions, even though it is not so definitely an army's function as that of waging war. But the question remains how this duty can be reconciled with that of providing an expeditionary force.

Now there is a fundamental difference between the qualities required for the first three functions and those required for the last. The development of automatic small arms and of mechanized mobility has increased the power of defence, and also the power of trained troops to quell insurrection. But an army in the field is still presumed to need the power of attack, in order to overcome the resistance of hostile troops with similar armament.

The additional armament, and the new types of it, which have been symbolically represented in recent exercises indicate the steps that are now being taken to resuscitate this moribund power. There are other means that may be tried, some of a less material nature. But will such developments suffice to overcome the existing superiority of the defensive, and its probable developments? Unless there is stronger reason than at present to think so, it might be wiser to modify prevailing ideas on the employment of the Army in a modern war. And to spend the money on equipment that will fit this modified role.

What does this reflection imply? At present, one clear factor in the problem is that the offensive is as much at an advantage in the air as it is at a disadvantage on land. This comparison, in conjunction with present deficiencies, has suggested that the offensive role, of an expeditionary force, might be entrusted to the Air Force. Apart from its greater promise of effect, it could be conducted from Britain's own shores or from bases more easy to secure and more remote from the enemy than the zone an army requires. And it would avoid many of the complications involved, and evolving, when an army is landed on the Continent.

The possibility of simplifying our military problems by such a redistribution of duties certainly deserves serious consideration. An essential preliminary is a thorough investigation, so far as practicable, of the prospects of reviving the power of the offensive on land. One deduction we can draw from the experience of the last war is that any attempt to restore it which is not radically different from the methods tried then is foredoomed to failure.

If it might be unwise at this stage to decide that the offensive activity of armies is beyond resurrection, that cannot be said of an interim arrangement in accord with the existing situation. One strong argument is that such a resurrection cannot yet be predicted with any assurance. A still stronger is that the British Army has not yet got the means to which its hopes are pinned. In the interval, it would seem more reasonable to entrust the old expeditionary role to the Air Force than to dream of sending an army into the field with new means that only exist in imagination.

The release of the Army at home from the precariously illimitable duty of providing a field force for the Continent would ensure that it was better able to fulfil its necessary duty as an Imperial Reserve. That purpose requires not only adequate numbers but a force which is thoroughly up-to-date, if not so heavily armed as would be required for the dubious attempt to force entrenched positions on the Continent.

This would seem the course best fitted to the existing realities of warfare on land. It will not suit those who desire the totalitarian training of the nation for war, as well as the preparation of a potentially unlimited army for intervention on the Continent. Since such ideas are growing in many circles, it is well to consider them at a time when cool reflection is possible, instead of under the stress of emergency. The haphazard way in which Britain's part in the Continental land struggle, with its exhausting demands, was determined in August, 1914, should be a warning to this generation.

To-day, owing to technical and tactical conditions, the despatch of a field army to the Continent does not seem to offer any promise of effect adequate to the risks involved. Since the blankness of the prospect is due to the inherent superiority of modern defence once this has had time to consolidate itself, it is hard to see that in preparing larger forces, to send still later, there is any greater prospect—except of greater waste of lives and resources. On the other hand, with a larger army the risk of its being hamstrung by air attack on its communications would be much increased. The advocates of a field force themselves recognize that the difficulties of transporting it and maintaining it overseas to-day would be much greater than in the past. And there is a further aspect to the problem. The more troops that are sent overseas the more shipping has to be diverted from the essential task of maintaining the supplies of the country, and the more targets are offered on the narrow sea passages—which are the most exposed to air and submarine attack. The problem of feeding the country in war is difficult enough without adding to the burden by superfluous and unpromising land campaigns on the Continent.

II

The Limitation of Arms

STUDY OF THE PROBLEM OF SECURITY, UNDER modern conditions and in present circumstances, tends to the conclusion that it is technically unattainable along customary lines. Augmentation of national armaments can no longer promise an adequate insurance even where superiority is possible. Any such superiority is apt to be far more fleeting than it was under past conditions: more easily forfeited by some technical development. Nor is that all that we have to consider. The incalculable factors in warfare have multiplied immensely. To evaluate forces and national degrees of security, in terms of numbers, is an obsolete convention. The instruments of warfare have become so intricate and their effects so hypothetical that the most profound calculation may prove no better than a guess in the dark. In the past, uncertainty turned mainly on the human factors; to-day the material factors magnify the uncertainty, and the men who handle them may become their sport. If the tendency of the time is towards turning men into robots, the machines themselves promise, or threaten, to produce a fresh variability.

While this may eventually frustrate any scheme of security, it has definitely upturned the old foundations. It is not in the nature of mankind to remain shelterless with content. Rebuilding must be attempted, so new ground must be sought. There are two courses, both converging to the same end. One is on the lines of collective security; the other on the lines of technical limitation—to limit the dangers from instruments that have already outstripped our powers of comprehension. It is easy to point out the uncertainty of either means, but difficult to suggest any alternative that is more than a mere acquiescence in, indeed a hastening of common devastation.

If, in experience, agreements have often been broken, that bare fact does not nullify their value. The more deeply one probes into historical records the more one comes to appreciate the restraining influence which agreements exercise. They operate both psychologically and technically. We are justified in deducing that assurances of help, prohibition of certain forms of action, and limitation of weapons, may be an effective check, if not a complete one. Their effect may even persist after they have been broken. Moreover, although each tie separately may seem a fragile strand, when interwoven they may form a powerful check.

It is important that each should be as definite as possible. The cause of peace has suffered much from idealists who, in their enthusiasm, put forward airy solutions that can be easily pricked by technical objections. And it would be a mistake for Governments to accept any prohibitions or limitations so wide that the unscrupulous can evade them—at the expense of those who keep the letter as well as the spirit of agreements. There is often more restraining power in the cumulative effect of a number of small but practicable checks than in a single sweeping measure formulated in vague terms.

From this point of view the proposals made by the German Government in May, 1935, appeared to have promise. They avoided the mistake of being too general, and the opposite mistake of defining each point too rigidly for adaptation in discussion. While the economic situation of Germany, together with the difficulties of quick-time production, may have had an influence on her willingness to accept limitation of the more expensive types of armament, the prospect of a race in such weapons is not to be welcomed elsewhere. Apart from the financial strain, the military advantage of a superiority is doubtful. It is too much like a race of indefinite extent for an unknown stake.

This reflection is emphasized if we consider the proposals in their bearing upon the military problems in Western Europe. A superiority in the size of warships and the calibre of naval guns is of very dubious advantage in the narrow seas. If theoretically possible on the assumption of a limitless purse, in reality its maintenance would be at the expense of the lighter craft needed for defence in these waters.

On land the technical arguments are no less strong for "abolition of the heaviest arms, especially suited for aggression"; these being the heavier artillery and heavier tanks. It has often been said that one cannot distinguish between offensive and defensive weapons. This is true—

if so loose a definition be used. All weapons are offensive, obviously, in the sense that they inflict injury, and all can be useful to the defence as well as to the attack. But not all can be as useful. Here is the crux: not that certain weapons are more offensive in themselves, but that they give a better chance, under modern conditions, of enabling attack to overcome defence. And so their abolition or limitation would at least promise a check on aggression by reducing the chances in favour of a would-be aggressor. In general it would increase the security offered by a fortified frontier. Though the risk might still remain of this being breached by some form of surprise, it would be a diminished risk. To circumscribe the chances is worth attempting, and the more so because the defensive is already superior to the offensive on land.

In the air it is otherwise, at the present time. The strongest check is the fear of prompt retaliation in superior force. Hence the importance of measures to ensure this by collective action. But it is also worth exploring subsidiary checks. Arguments for outlawing certain methods of war, such as the bombing of the civil population, have more support in experience than they may have in pure logic. The laws that were broken in the last war had, on the whole, more restraining force than the public appreciated. It may prove difficult to fulfil, or even to frame, an effective prohibition of "the dropping of gas, incendiary, and explosive bombs outside the real battle zone", but before dismissing the conception its practicable adaptation may well be considered. The unlimited horrors of the Thirty Years War produced an effective limitation of methods by common consent in the century and a half that followed. That example might be repeated. The experience of the last war and the omens of the next unite in a warning of what otherwise awaits us. Practical wisdom may restrain what strict logic unleashes.

Military Training

MILITARY TRAINING, WHETHER UNDER HIS-
torical or under psychological analysis, is found to be
divided into two spheres, a higher and a lower—the
training of the commander and the training of those
who act under command. In the actual practice of training the division has often been ignored or confused, especially in the early preparation of future leaders. The
consequence has too often been their ultimate stultifica-
tion as leaders. This is shown in the rarity of inspired
and creative leadership in the organized armies of history. Generals have been legion; artists of war few.
Many more, and infinitely greater military genius can be
traced in the scantier records of irregular and guerilla
forces. The natural explanation is that the natural gifts
of these leaders who have emerged straight from the
womb of conflict, instead of a professional incubation
chamber, have not been cramped or warped by convention. To acknowledge the genius of many of these irregular leaders does not imply that they would have been
equally successful if placed in command of a more highly
organized type of force, at any rate until they had

gained experience of its organization and different application. But it does cast a reflection upon the customary
method of training leaders in organized armies. It is significant that in the American Civil War, which was the
most fruitful field of generalship in modern times, most
of the outstanding leaders were men who after an apprenticeship in the Regular Army had gone into some
field of civil activity, which in varying degree freed their
minds from the fetters of military convention and
routine, while they retained a useful experience of the
functioning of the military machine.

The adage that it is necessary to learn to obey before
one can command, although it contains an element of
truth, has been greatly abused in its actual application to
the education of leaders. There has been too little differ-
entiation in it between the spirit of obedience to a
common purpose and the mechanical form of obedience.
Many of the greatest military leaders have shown themselves exceptionally restive in their early career under
the restraints of conventional discipline. One may cite
the candid confessions of Grant and Sherman as to their
behaviour when cadets at West Point, and their critical
reflections in old age on the system of training to which
they had been subjected in youth. In British history, such
men as Wolfe, Wellington, and Nelson showed themselves even less amenable to the outward forms of discipline. It is only too evident that these and many others
became great leaders not because of but rather in spite of
their early training—because, instead, their personalities
were too strong to be forced into the conventional
groove. Thus there is unconscious humour in the fact

that such men have been held up as exemplars to the young officers of later generations who were undergoing the same kind of training. Only ignorance of history, or excess of varnish, can explain such unwitting irony. If there are signs of change in the military educational system, a much greater change is needed, and a much clearer distinction, before schools for officers can truly be regarded as an aid towards preparing officers for leadership. That change must be towards the university ideal of education, of training young men to think for themselves, instead of moulding their minds to a sealed pattern.

The obvious difficulty, of course, in the solution of this problem of military education is that officers, although in all grades called upon to exercise command, have also to act under command except in the highest grades. But the problem is not so difficult as it may seem so long as the system of education is based on a true understanding of the spirit of discipline, and the system of discipline is elastic rather than rigid.

THE TRAINING OF THE SOLDIER

The training of those who simply act under command, and merely handle the inanimate tools of war, is a simpler problem. Not so simple as it used to be before weapons became complex mechanisms and before their long-range effect compelled the dispersion of the combatants on the battlefield, but still simple in comparison with the training of a leader.

The object of the soldier's training is threefold. To make him skilled in handling his weapons under battle conditions. To make him an interlocking and frictionless cog in the military machine, which implies the development of automatic obedience, of instinctive combination according to some practised system of action, and of physical stamina. Thirdly, and above all, to make him conquer his own sense of fear.

Military exercises and military discipline have been the two main agencies used to produce the trained soldier. But they have had a purely moral accompaniment in the cultivation of a distinctive military spirit—springing from comradeship and bound up by the strands of *esprit de corps*.

The form of military exercises has naturally varied with the changing nature of weapons and the consequent changes in the fighting formation of military bodies. These exercises may be classified as individual and collective. In their application to the training of the soldier both classes have in the past been predominantly, and still are to a large extent, based upon drill—that is, the repetition of certain movements until their performance becomes instinctive. If such drill has the primary purpose of developing working efficiency, it has also been of use, especially in the past, as a supplement to discipline and the military spirit. By a discipline of the muscles the reflexes of obedience were developed so that the soldier could continue to act effectively even when his mind was numbed by fear.

Military discipline, in the strait sense of the term, is the enforcement of instant obedience to orders through the threat of punishment, supplemented by the control of the reflexes established through drill. In the wider sense it is bound up with the soldierly spirit. So far as this is susceptible to analysis, its components appear to be the pride of manhood, the pride of arms (of being an initiate in the martial cult), the confidence that comes from skill at arms, the sense of comradeship, the sense of duty, and the sense of loyalty—to comrades, commander, corps and country.

The proportions of these components have certainly varied. Thus in the citizen-military armies of the Greek city-states and the Roman Republic, patriotism would seem to have been the dominant element—at any rate in the willing soldier's spirit. The same has been true of the armies of the French Revolution and of the "national" armies subsequently. In the army of ancient Sparta, the influence of its martial cult would seem to have risen to at least equal proportions with patriotism. In the Roman legions from the time of Marius onwards patriotism counted for little, and personal loyalty to a commander took its place. It was in the early part of the first century B.C. that the old oath of allegiance sworn annually was replaced by a personal and permanent oath of loyalty to the commander. As for the mystical sense of membership of a cult we can see its power in Cæsar's ability to quell a mutiny by addressing his men as *quirites* or civilians.

These two elements continued to be predominant throughout the Middle Ages, first in the feudal forces, then in the "free companies" who hired themselves out collectively, and later in the swelling volume of mercenaries who enlisted in the army of any sovereign willing to pay them.

When standing armies became general, from the

seventeenth century onward, the element of personal loyalty to the general declined in importance, to be succeeded by loyalty to the corps—the regimental spirit. Patriotism naturally revived as a motive factor when armies were raised from natives of the country. Yet in all professional armies the martial cult and *esprit de corps* have remained as powerful influences on the soldier's spirit.

No student of war is likely to underrate the strength of the military spirit as a cement to armies, especially those whose ranks are filled with men of some intelligence. Yet, equally, no scientific historian will fail to perceive how much of their fighting power and fortitude especially in the past, was due to a severely punitive discipline, which inspired a fear that overcame fear of the enemy.

Spartan discipline is proverbial, yet it had a larger moral element in its application than that of most armies until recent times. Those who ran away were punished by shame—they could hold no office, could receive no wife, were exposed to insult or blows without the right of reply, were compelled to wear patched and particoloured dress, and were only allowed to shave one side of their faces.

Roman discipline, in comparison, was far more physical in its deterrents, the death penalty being frequently inflicted. When a body of troops failed in the hour of battle, a customary punishment was decimation—the putting to death of every tenth man. But it is interesting to note that the Romans subtly appealed to the military spirit in some of their disciplinary measures, by giving them the semblance of punishment for a crime against comradeship and the corps rather than merely against the state. Thus the delinquents were punished by a form of running the gauntlet in which the other soldiers of the legion, armed with sticks and stones, normally battered them to death. On the other hand, the Romans, as an off-set to these merciless penalties, created a regular system of rewards for distinguished service, apart from the ordinary incentive of loot.

We find the Roman practice of decimation revived by Wallenstein in 1642 to punish a regiment which had led the flight from the battlefield. If the enforcement of discipline varied greatly in the armies of the seventeenth century, the scale of punishments were very severe. In that of Gustavus, however, they were employed as much to ensure good behaviour in quarters as bravery in battle. And the Swedish Army was certainly a shining contrast to the marauding armies of the day in its conduct towards the people of the territory it passed through. In Marlborough's army discipline was tightened, running the gauntlet and, for lesser crimes, whipping being the chief forms of punishment. The rod, however, was now used to punish many offences for which death or mutilation had formerly been inflicted. In 1712 there was a case of a soldier being sentenced to 12,600 stripes in seven applications.

It was left to Frederick the Great to produce the most severely drilled and disciplined army that the world has perhaps yet known, with the calculated purpose of turning men into automatic machines that could fire five volleys a minute—with a flint lock musket!—while ad-

vancing and manœuvring at a slow march under the
enemy's fire, and that could be relied on to keep up these
rolling volleys while their rigidly dressed ranks were
being torn by bullets and cannon balls. It was a triumph
of merciless discipline and drill over human nature. Blind
obedience was the keynote of a system in which the
death penalty was introduced for the soldier who even
dared to grumble at his sergeant's exacting orders.

It was only by comparison that other armies seemed
less severely disciplined. Thus in the British Army and
Navy the cat-o'-nine-tails, superseding the rod, reigned
throughout the eighteenth and far into the nineteenth
century, as the regular penalty for offences great and
small—a hundred lashes being regarded as quite natural
for the latter, and anything up to fifteen hundred for the
former. We learn that in the 28th Foot in 1806 any man
who failed to pass the inspecting officer's scrutiny of his
turn-out was flogged on the spot, and that from ten to
twenty men used to be punished at a single parade. If
some commanding officers were reluctant to flog, the
power was grossly abused by many. Not until the Royal
Commission of 1835 was a systematic limitation imposed,
and not until 1881 was flogging finally abolished. Every
effort towards reform had been fiercely opposed by
senior officers who declared that any limitation would
ruin the discipline of the Army.

We should recognize that the men in the ranks were
largely composed of the scourings of the slums, so that
some excuse may be found in their vicious tendencies for
the drastic measures taken to ensure good behaviour. We
must recognize that so long as men fought in close for-

mations—from the Spartan phalanx of spears down to the serried lines of Frederick's grenadiers—wherein each man must move in dovetailed uniformity with his neighbours to ensure cohesion, there was a military value in a discipline and drill that turned men into machines.

It was as much due to the growing effect of firearms, which compelled looser formations, as to a growing humanity that in the nineteenth century the methods of discipline became gradually less severe. Even so, old habits die hard and even in the armies of the early twentieth century discipline remained predominantly punitive as a means of subduing the independent will of the soldier and as a means, perhaps overrated, of enabling him to face danger through the conscious or subconscious fear of the more certain penalties that awaited him if he failed. Even to-day there are military students who maintain that instinctive courage is so weak and self-respect so unsafe a support that it is wiser to impose courage through the impress of a martinet discipline.

Yet a different way was introduced, and vindicated, more than a century ago in what is known as Sir John Moore's system of training. Its origin was partly tactical, partly humane. The more intelligent British officers who fought in America were impressed by the impracticability of pitting stiff-ranked formations against the forest craft of the Red Indians, and the need of combating them with a new type of resourceful light infantry. On Christmas Day, 1755, took place the birth of a corps, the 60th Royal Americans (now the King's Royal Rifle Corps), which became a light to the whole military world. It developed not only a new style of infantry tactics, but under Colonel Bouquet, a new form of discipline, in which the self-respect and self-confidence of the men was fostered by an atmosphere of trust and brutality replaced by sympathy. In preference to imposed discipline there was a cultivation of all the elements of the soldierly spirit to the end that men should acquire self-control. The experience of the American Revolution and the hard lessons taught by the colonists acted as a spur to this new tendency, and eventually led, first, to the formation of the Experimental Rifle Corps in 1800, and then to the training of the Light Brigade at Shorncliffe under Sir John Moore. It gave a new spiritual meaning to discipline and added a moral to a merely physical cohesion with results that were proved in the Peninsular War, where the Light Division was the salt of the Army.

Its triumphs were the more remarkable because the salt was damped, the light dimmed, by many conservative soldiers who lacked the insight and the courage to place their trust in the new system. This adulteration continued in the generations that followed, although partially offset by the rising level of humanity in the people at large. At the present day, one can say that the methods of discipline, if not its spirit, are virtually equivalent to those of Sir John Moore's system. But they should have made a century's progress. By comparison with the immense change in the customs of civil life, we can see that there is far too much stress on physical deterrents even in the most enlightened codes of military discipline. And too little emphasis on intelligence. Today the revolutionary changes in warfare point the urgent need of a fresh change in discipline. The increasingly mechanical nature of weapons demands the intellectual development of the men who handle them—at any rate of those who act individually or in little groups. When battle was waged essentially between physical bodies there was a value in turning men into machines. Now that battle is being waged more and more between machines the object of military training should be to produce men who will be masters of the machine—by developing their mental powers.

THE TRAINING OF THE COMMANDER

If executive intelligence is becoming more and more needed in the soldier, creative intelligence is and always has been the supreme requirement in the commander—coupled with moral courage. War is a two-party affair, and thus conventionality of thought inevitably tends to confirm this equality of kind, conducing to stalemate. The best hope of tilting the scales and of overcoming the resistance inherent in conflict lies in originality—to produce something unexpected that will paralyze the opponent's freedom of action.

But, in historical fact, such creative intelligence has been rare in the operations of war. And rarer still in preparation for war. Military history is filled with the record of military improvements that have been resisted by those who would have profited richly from them. Between the development of new weapons or new tactics and their adoption there has always been a time-lag, often of generations. And that time-lag has often decided the fate of nations.

The explanation lies not only in the system of training

but in a psychological attitude underlying it. The officer has never been taught to approach his problems, and the investigation of experience, in a spirit of scientific enquiry. His early training is directed, above all, to the cultivation of unquestioning loyalty—multiple loyalties—to sovereign, country, service, corps and his superiors. To strengthen him for his fighting function, and for the tremendous trials of fortitude this entails, the development of an intense spirit of loyalty has great value. But, obviously, it becomes an obstacle when the man so brought up turns to investigate the facts of warfare. His compound loyalties create prejudices which inevitably colour his vision and bias his judgment. They may be essential to the soldier in action, but they are a hindrance in reflection—where facts should be analyzed in a scientific spirit, with complete detachment from all loyalties save that to truth. To understand this fundamental difficulty of the military mind not only helps to explain its historical records of myopia but may help many who feel bitter at the consequences to judge the case more charitably.

But charity does not imply contentment. It may be that only a philosopher could reconcile the opposing loyalties harmoniously, but something could be done to help the normal soldier in adapting himself to the conflicting roles of loyal executant in war and truth-loyal student of war. The first need is a change of attitude towards criticism and independence of thought. It would be helped if there was a recognition of the psychological commonplace that men of personality and originality—in other words, the men naturally fitted to be leaders —are inherently critical. And in fact the great leaders of the past who are taken as examples were critically minded. A second need is for a new attitude to knowledge, and the encouragement of a spirit of enquiry. Satisfaction with present knowledge is the chief bar to the pursuit of knowledge. It has been so in all branches and professions. If the military profession is no worse than others, that is no just cause for contentment. Nor does the history of armies yield any cause for self-satisfaction to any soldier who digs down into it. In these conditions lack of criticism is a proof of virgin ignorances. Those who have studied war the most cannot avoid becoming acutely conscious that the exploration of war as a scientific subject has scarcely been begun.

SOCIAL EFFECTS OF MILITARY TRAINING

These can be summarized briefly, or otherwise require a comprehensive historical survey, not possible here. The effects have naturally been far-reaching wherever compulsory military service has been the custom. They have been correspondingly insignificant save indirectly among those peoples who have depended upon mercenaries or upon permanent professional forces, as separation from the normal life of the people naturally tends to give the soldier a sense of isolation that in time accentuates the natural caste spirit arising from pride of arms and the mystical bond of comradeship between men who have faced danger together.

The physical benefit of military training is very marked, so long as it is accompanied by good feeding and housing conditions. Its value, however, lies in the open-air life and exercise rather than in the specific forms of military drill, which are certainly inferior to gymnastic exercises. This can be seen in the present Italian army where open-air gymnastics and physical training are carried out extensively. The physical development and activity of the men who have done their military service is remarkable.

The moral benefit of military training varies with the system of discipline in vogue. It is highest when the predominant emphasis is placed on an appeal to the soldierly spirit, and lowest when unthinking obedience is imposed through fear of the consequences. The purely punitive form has little more than a negative value and then only as applied to the lowest form of manhood. In contrast the elements which make up the soldierly spirit are in proportion to their development a foundation of good citizenship.

The mental benefit is more doubtful, save in so far as it provides opportunity for practising leadership or for developing specialized knowledge. Military training certainly tends to stimulate quickness of thought. On the other hand, it inevitably tends to uniformity of thought, if this may be relieved by the diverse tests and intense experiences of active service.

These influences together with the educational facilities that now commonly exist in an army may contribute to a definite increase of mental capacity in a backward community or when applied to backward types of men. In Russia, for example, the idea of using the army as a lever through which to raise the intellectual level of the masses lies at the base of a noteworthy educational experiment.

The wider effects of military training upon society, and the political effects, can be gauged in past history. Thus in the city-states of Greece, whose armies were citizen militias, it seems reasonably clear that the duty of military service did not harm the intellectual development of their finest minds, while it undoubtedly strengthened the sense of citizenship. Moreover, the restriction of military service to free citizens tended to enhance its moral significance. Decay began when, under the strain of the long-drawn Peloponnesian war, slaves and mercenaries were enlisted. On the other hand, it is clear that the drawbacks of military training outweighed the advantages in the case of Sparta, where the nation was turned into the equivalent of a military corps, and the unmarried men lived entirely in barracks. The civilization of Sparta was stunted and the poorness of its contribution to the intellectual and artistic achievements of ancient Greece is only to be explained by its military "life" as a nation.

If early Rome was almost barren in the arts, its highly developed civic virtues and its contribution to political science cannot, in analysis, be separated from its system of military service. Under the Tullian organization the army comprised all citizens from seventeen to sixty years of age, those under forty-seven being used for service in the field. They were enrolled for a year at a time which, in normal practice, meant a summer's campaign only. But the expansion of "empire" which followed the Punic wars broke down the old citizen levy system. Marius abolished the restriction of service to men of some property, and from that time onward the army became professional and long-service, with an increasing dependence on the men of subject races and eventually on alien "barbarians". If the change assisted the growth of civilization in Rome, it unquestionably contributed to the decline and fall of Roman civilization.

In modern times also, notably in the eighteenth century, the discontinuance of the duty of military service, and the consequent dependence of states upon an isolated military caste, can be seen to have paved the way to disaster. Sometimes it has been internal, through the overthrow of a government by a minority who alone possessed and knew how to use the lever of force. More often, it has been external, as when the professionally dependent states of Europe were overthrown by the national armies of Revolutionary France.

The latter danger is reduced with the scientific development of weapons that makes mere numbers of small account. The former danger remains, as may be seen in the state of Germany to-day. This danger is reduced where there is a militia system, voluntary or otherwise, as well as a professional army.

But beyond these deductions, it is too early to make any prediction as to the social effects of abandoning or continuing compulsory military training in civilized states of advanced civilization.

13

The Higher Direction of Forces

IN EXPLORING THE HISTORY OF 1914-18, THE impression grows that the personal performance of commanders was often far better than its actual effect. Many of the attacks that have been levied against them miss the real point by overlooking this difference. It was to a large extent the natural consequence of the conditions which bounded the exercise of high command in a war of masses. The remoteness of the higher commanders from the battlefield made it even more difficult for them to gauge the real situation there than it was for them to influence that situation. Whereas in Napoleon's time it had been true to say that the best general was the one who made the fewest mistakes, it was nearer the truth now that the best general was the one who caused the least mistakes. Actual command was split into myriad fragments, resting in the hands of the company and platoon leaders: the higher commanders had changed into company directors. Deprived of personal experience of battlefield reality, they were handicapped in correcting the inevitable discrepancies of pre-war theory: in checking the theory with the facts, and in adjusting it to the new developments.

It is not easy to determine the effect of recent developments on this 1914–18 condition, but the present probability is that this psychological remoteness may be increased in more ways than it is decreased, at any rate in the sphere of the higher command. And it may be further complicated by the freshness of the problems which confront the local commanders of the new-pattern forces. Mechanization is inevitable; the European country that places its faith in old means and methods might find its faith even more misplaced than was that of the Abyssinians, who had the asset of a remote mountain fastness. Yet mechanization carries with it risks that it would be foolish to ignore. Chief among them is not food-supply but mind-supply.

There is serious cause to doubt whether we shall find sufficient officers capable of directing and handling these high-mobility forces until a new generation, born in the motor age, has grown up. And without the necessary mental adjustment to the new conditions, chaos may result when these forces are launched against those of a similar type. The Italians suffered serious congestion and disorganization in the early months of their campaign, yet they had no modern opponent equipped with aircraft and landcraft to make that confusion worse confounded. The dangers of inadequate mental adjustment have been increased by the years of delay in beginning the process of mechanization and in providing the means of training. For unless there has been time to develop a mechanically mobile sense in peace-time, we are inviting breakdown if we have to attempt a hurried transformation under the stress of war.

But the problems that call for attention go far beyond the sphere of mechanization. In Britain, this has been recognized by the latest edition of *Field Service Regulations*, which emphasizes that high command in war requires:

"The broadest possible outlook and knowledge, of social as well as of military questions. War is now more than ever a social problem: a major war affects the whole of the national life and every class of citizen, and there is a corresponding civil influence on the conduct of military operations."

There is also an essential similarity between the principles or common-sense precepts which lead to success in war and those which govern any affairs where active opposition or competition has to be overcome. Both the military commander and the ordinary citizen who is planning a business transaction have to take into their calculations the possible schemes of rivals. Too many military plans have broken down through the failure to realize that war is essentially a two-party affair. The very principle of concentration, that was so continually on the lips of the dominant soldiers in 1914–18, becomes meaningless unless the enemy's concentration is prevented by well-devised distractions, which require detachments from your own. Applied without comprehension, this "principle" too often proved in practice no better than an unpractical catchword. Its dangers emphasize the importance of imagination—to put oneself in the enemy's shoes and to see things from other points of view. Nor-

mal service training in peace-time has hitherto done little
to develop such qualities, or the habit of applying them.

While the new British *Field Service Regulations* emphasizes the fundamental similarity between the qualities
required for military and civil leadership it suggests,
more questionably, that a difference arises owing to the
fact that "the conditions of war are utterly unfamiliar
to the ordinary civilized man". It may well be asked
what opportunity the professional soldier has in peace-
time to become familiar with the stresses of battle. Past
experience he may have, but so now have millions of
civilians. But even this may be of little service as accli-
matization for the conditions of a new war. A better
ground for arguing the regular soldier's advantage over
the ordinary citizen is that he becomes so habituated to
military processes that he can perform them instinctively
in the heat of action, so that his functional efficiency is
apt to be less affected by the "friction" of war. Here,
undoubtedly, is a real asset.

It applies, however, in far less degree to the higher
sphere of war, where it may be outweighed by handicaps
that are inevitable in peace-time soldiering. The poli-
tician is always "at war", and the business man commonly in competition with others. They have constant
practice in conflict, and unceasing experience of its psychological conditions. Soldiering, in comparison, is a shel-
tered occupation save in war. The ease with which the
will of the superior prevails inside an army becomes a
handicap in preparation for dealing with a hostile army.
Always revolving between the poles of authority and
obedience, the soldier gains little or no psychological ex-

perience as a fighter. Exercises in mimic war, regulated by umpires, cannot compare with the exacting tests of the political or the business field.

An appreciation of these conditions may arouse sympathy for the generals of the last war who, from the isolation of a headquarter office, had to direct armies of millions composed of the people in arms, and were pitted against an active foe in a warfare which embraced a diversity of factors that were military only by adoption. There is no cause for surprise that they failed so often to gauge their steps, or the enemy's; rather is it remarkable, when all is weighed, that they adapted themselves even as well as they did to conditions for which they were, by training and environment, so little prepared.

Yet this reflection leads to another, on the way that square pegs were placed in round holes. Although it was a war of nations, and many of the best brains of the nations were drawn into the forces, they were excluded from those military spheres in which "the broadest possible outlook and knowledge" were needed. The custom of all the forces erected the principle that no one was fit to have a voice in matters of strategy unless he had nearly forty years' experience of the military machine. It was certainly a novel principle, since it would have excluded nearly all the great commanders of history, from Alexander, Hannibal and Cæsar, down to Cromwell, Marlborough and Napoleon. And it was the more strange since the twentieth century strategist had to deal with many more non-military factors. But although the principle flew in the face of historical experience and modern knowledge, the records show that it was rigidly maintained—except in the Australian and Canadian forces —throughout the four years of war.

By a practical paradox, the civilian was invited to take over the most strictly professional functions of soldiering while he was viewed as an intruder in the higher and hence less technical posts. Any intelligent citizen with administrative experience found it easy to master the details of staff-work—as soon as he had "learnt the language" his past experience here became a strong asset. In comparison, it was far more difficult for him to become an efficient regimental officer. Proficiency in the operative technique of an infantry or artillery unit, in a regular army, is the product of habit as well as of specialized training.

The higher the plane of war, the more the solution of its problems depends on wide knowledge, broad outlook, and depth of thought: and the less, comparatively, on technical experience. This does not mean that knowledge of military technique is unnecessary: without it, the ablest man would be handicapped, especially in dealing with forces which have a long-established system of operation. The principles of fighting are based on common-sense, but something more is needed to apply them effectively in the handling of armies. The better a man's mental equipment, however, the less time he will take to acquire an adequate knowledge of such technique. And in acquiring it quickly he will have an advantage over the man who has taken thirty or forty years in climbing the military ladder. Instruments and methods will have changed, and often be entirely new, since the other man served his apprenticeship to arms. It is difficult for the older soldier to have a sure grasp of weapons he has never handled, and of methods he has never carried out. Moreover, if his technical experience lies several steps back, it becomes more difficult for him to gauge the next step forward. What he gains by having prolonged experience of command may be offset by lacking first-hand knowledge of the present tools of command.

Nevertheless it was only in the Dominion Forces that the F.S.R. definition had a chance of test. Its results are significant. Since technical proficiency and executive habit count for more in the lower grades, it is to be inferred that a non-professional soldier who proved himself barely the equal of many regulars as a battalion or brigade commander might prove outstanding when, and if, he reached a higher command. That inference was confirmed by actual experience in the Dominion Forces, notably in the case of General Monash.

When the conditions of the war are analyzed, it becomes clear that in the qualifications for high command, and still more for strategic direction, there was little in pre-war professional experience that helped a man, while there was much that might handicap the development of his personal qualities. One important qualification remained which could not be quickly acquired; the man who had spent a lifetime in the military profession might here have had a special advantage. An objective study of the past would have been a guide to the conditions that were in development. But for such study professional soldiers had no training and limited opportunity. The discovery of uncomfortable facts had never been encouraged in armies, who treated their history as

a sentimental treasure rather than a field of scientific research. Thus the potential asset was left a "buried talent".

All were amateurs in that war from the moment when
the opening moves broke down, and the real nature of
the war emerged from the artificial mould of convention
in which the pre-war plans and forces had been cast.
The question which remained was how quickly they
could learn, and whether their minds could expand to
the scale of the problems. The chances of this adaptation,
as well as the opportunity for fresh minds, were diminished by a delusion—that they were professionals in the
larger sphere.

In retrospect, it can hardly be considered that the results were satisfactory, or that the power of adaptation
equalled the need. The question remains whether it will
be adequate if another emergency comes, under conditions that are still more complex, even less "military" and
far more difficult to gauge. At present there is small reason to expect a different result to that of 1914–18. It
would seem essential both to give professional minds
greater opportunity for development and to make more
use of other minds. Here is a problem that is inseparable
from all calculation of what is "an adequate standard" of
defence.

14

The Higher Education of Officers

IS THERE ANY SOLUTION FOR THE PROBLEM outlined in the previous chapter? An obvious one is to raise the standard of intelligence and education required of the prospective officer, but its achievement is not easy. In Britain the question of the education and training of officers was examined in 1924 by a committee under Lord Haldane's chairmanship, which included two of the ablest soldiers then in the War Office as well as a leading member, and future Vice-Chancellor, of Cambridge University, Mr. Will Spens. That Committee pointed out that the problem had two aspects: "It is much to be desired that first-rate brains should be attracted into the Army. It is not necessary, nor is it wholly desirable, that all, or even the majority, of regimental officers should be intellectuals. . . . In consequence, a very difficult problem has to be solved in part by attracting a certain number of boys of high intellectual ability and in securing the proper opportunities of further education for these, and for the rest by attracting and educating a large number of boys in regard to whom stress is laid on character rather than on high intellectual qualifications." The Committee also declared that "any adequate improvement in the quality and quantity of candidates must depend upon a larger number of parents being induced to regard the Army as an attractive career for their sons. This implies the necessity of convincing parents that the Army provides openings for brains and character comparable with those provided in the Civil Service or in the other professions. The task of convincing parents may in the end become a matter of propaganda; but propaganda will be valueless unless the system can fairly be said to have been so adjusted as to make it true that such openings exist in fact. Nor is this all. Conviction is only likely to be secured on a sufficient scale by changes in the present system, which will not only provide such openings, but which will also make them sufficiently striking to attract attention.

"It has been represented to us by the many authorities that we have consulted that if it is desired to make the Army attractive as a profession to men of good intellectual attainments, certain conditions are essential: (1) Work must be provided of sufficient intellectual interest. (2) There must be real opportunities for advancement by merit. (3) The remuneration must be adequate."

Besides emphasizing that a genuine system of promotion by merit was "essential" if the officer corps was "to be prevented from stagnating", the report suggested that university candidates should be given special facilities for entering the Staff College early in their service and that the system of proficiency pay should be extended much beyond its existing limits, to encourage the acquirement of special knowledge of some particular military or scientific subject.

The Committee, in conclusion, stated: "We attach the greatest importance to the whole question of providing at every stage adequate rewards for exceptional capacity. We believe liberal provision in this direction to be essential with a view to encouraging able boys to become officers, and we are unanimous in our opinion that a great opportunity exists at the present time to initiate the suggested reforms. It is not too late to convince the public that the lessons of the war are being taken seriously to heart by the military authorities, and that it is their firm intention to make the Army an attractive career for men of talent. If we wait much longer the public will feel that the Army is such a hopelessly conservative institution that no vital change is possible in the principles on which the post-war Army is organized."

More than a dozen years have passed since the Haldane Committee made its report. Its concrete recommendations have been fulfilled only in small degree, and its intentions still less. For adequate effect, in attracting "first-rate brains" to the Army, it would be necessary not only to offer greater inducements but to dispel longstanding assumptions, both within and without the military sphere. We should have to change the way that the Army looks at itself, and also the way it is regarded by the outside world. While certain improvements have been made in the education and training of officers, none would seem to have gone far enough to fulfil the Committee's condition of being "sufficiently striking" to attract attention and carry conviction—of an adequate change. Schoolmasters, in general, have tended to view with pained surprise any boy of scholarship standard who expressed the intention of entering the Army, and to deplore such a waste of his gifts. And in most public schools where an "army class" existed it has not stood high in the estimation of the boys themselves, being commonly regarded as the refuge of those who have more brawn than brain. Only a few years ago a headmaster candidly told a soldier who was seeking his aid in improving the supply of officers: "I only advise boys who would be quite impossible in any other walk of life to go to Sandhurst"—the British equivalent to West Point. The effect of an opinion so wide-spread and long-standing has naturally been to keep the standard of recruitment low, and, naturally also, the opinion was extended rather than changed by the experience of the last war when the army absorbed the nation, and the "old boys" who came into the army for the duration of the emergency found themselves in subordination—permanently, and not merely while they were serving their apprenticeship to arms—to the low-rated "army class" of their schooldays. Only a dynamic proof of professional efficiency could have altered such an old-established view—and that, in general, was hardly forthcoming.

In some ways the military profession, if it tenaciously maintained its claims to privilege while the war lasted, has been more ready than most to abandon its preconceptions. That progress is apt to be concealed by a habit of "trade-union" loyalty which leads its members to deny publicly, often in tones of the utmost indignation,

the faults they not merely admit but castigate privately
—soldiers are rarely true to their better selves in public
speeches. But since the war there has been a remarkable
concurrence of opinion among the heads of the British
Army on the need to broaden the basis of military education, and although suggestions differ on the means of
achieving this object, they all have a "University" key-
note. The old prejudice against officers who entered the
Army through the Universities instead of through the
Military Colleges has disappeared, and been replaced by
a desire to obtain as many as possible. Under present
conditions, however, the supply is limited; partly because of the greater cost to parents of this mode of entry;
partly because the career has not been sufficiently attractive to young men capable of taking a good degree.
Even now, the antedate given to University candidates
is so limited that a man who has taken first-class honours
starts at no advantage, even at a disadvantage, in senior-
ity compared with the cadet who has passed through
Sandhurst. Until this is changed we can hardly expect
more candidates from the Universities, or those candidates to be of the best.

As an alternative there has been an effort to widen
the educational basis of the Royal Military College at
Sandhurst, and to remodel the system on university lines.
Addressing the Headmasters' Conference in 1930, the
Chief Instructor at Sandhurst frankly said on the subject
of these changes:

"Warfare was becoming more and more complicated,
requiring brains and ability of the officers, and we found
that we had to build up the brains and personalities of

the officers from the very beginning. We realized that in the Great War some of the greatest mistakes of officers were made in their dealings with civilians and in their lack of knowledge of civilians, and we realized that a great war needed broadmindedness on the part of its leaders.

"The old regime at Sandhurst aimed at turning out purely military specialists, and this was not what the Army or the public wanted. The curriculum which was going on undoubtedly deadened a boy's intellect and led his thoughts into narrow channels. A boy was asked to have an active mind when his body was really exhausted. He was never taught to think out things for himself. We made him spend hours taking his rifle to bits and still more hours putting it together again.

"The Sandhurst curriculum has to be drastically overhauled, and in the new curriculum we now try to give a boy the power of self-development."

Where the object of old was to turn out a cadet who on joining his regiment would be a perfectly trained private soldier—it was even laid down that there was to be no attempt to train him as a leader—the aim is now to give him an idea of the elements of leadership and some practical opportunity of exercising it; weapon-training has been reduced to an outline knowledge, and general subjects increased in variety, while teaching in class has been supplemented by providing more time for private study.

Through these changes there has been a marked improvement in the educational value of a Sandhurst course. Yet the closer approach to the University system has tended to emphasize the gulf which separates the intellectual atmosphere of a military college from that which characterizes a university. It is easy to provide company officers who are good sportsmen, but difficult to find instructors who combine deep knowledge with the ability to create a thirst for it. It is still more difficult to develop the power of independent thought in an establishment steeped in the traditions of military discipline. Thus, despite the enthusiasm shown in pursuing this aim, the result has fallen short of the original hopes.

There has been, partly in consequence, a recent revival of the suggestion that the military colleges should be abolished and entry into the Army be entirely through the Universities. For this system to produce the required number of officers it would, of course, be necessary to subsidize the University course of accepted candidates. Even so, the cost would be an inconsiderable fraction of the Army budget, a fraction so small that if viewed with a sense of proportion it should not weigh against the prospective benefit.

The trend of modern warfare gives ever-increasing point to this suggestion, as a University offers a broader educational basis and also more opportunity for specialized study, both of which are needed to meet the growing complexity of warfare and its tendency to be more and more influenced by non-military factors. Again, to make entry through the University general would help to diminish the difference of outlook, as distinct from a difference of ability, between officers who are likely to stay at regimental duty and those who may be employed in the higher direction of forces.

Modern warfare demands an ever greater power of adjustment to new conditions; the effect of the higher direction may be paralyzed unless the executants also acquire an increased degree of mental adaptability.

Another potential advantage of a general University entry might be in offering the means of fulfilling one of the most important recommendations of the Haldane Committee:

"It is desirable in every profession to have a foundational basis on which the insight of those who practise it rests. To change the metaphor, it is always helpful to the practitioner, old or young, to have a background for his reasoning against which he can set or estimate it. For the physicist, pure mathematics performs this role, for the student of philosophy, the history of past systems is the background against which he sets and estimates his ideas; for the physician, physiology and pathology give him what he needs of this kind, just as anatomy gives it for the surgeon. Is there any subject which can bring the study of military strategy and tactics into a relation with life in yet wider aspects in such a way as to illuminate that study, render it more interesting, and develop not only its significance, but the direction in it which must be looked for in new ideas?

"We believe that the study of military history in a wider and less restricted form than has hitherto been current in establishments for military education may do a great deal in this direction. The strategy of a particular nation must always be in large measure the outcome of its geographical conditions and of its history. Great Britain and the British Empire consist largely of posses-

sions surrounded or in large measure bounded by the
sea. Their military history has therefore been based on
sea-power. This fact has exercised a dominating influence
on British strategy and on British history. Apart from
this history and the strategical necessities which it has
disclosed neither the science nor the art of British warfare are intelligible. They require an intelligent and comprehensive study of history to bring out their meaning,
and to guide the officer in his military studies. With
France and Germany the conditions and the histories
have naturally been quite different, and the study of
them, while very valuable from a general standpoint,
cannot take the place of that of British military institu-
tions, and of the fashion in which with us land-power is
conditioned by sea-power."

Such a truly educative use of military history has not
proved possible under the present system. It demands,
in the first place, the study of books which treat the subject scientifically instead of sentimentally: as history,
not as a pleasantly flavoured fairy tale or an uplifting
moral story. Books of the former kind are rare in this
field; there has been little encouragement to produce
them. It demands, in the second place, the development
of a critical mind in the student; to this there has been
even less encouragement. A few instructors, inspired by
the university ideal, have done their best to bring it into
the military colleges, but their effect has been over-
borne by the weight of authority—well-meaning but
uncomprehending, saturated in pious traditions, and
anxious lest discipline might be impaired or respect for
superiors disturbed. Armies are temples of ancestor-

worship. It is not necessary to depreciate the moral help
they gain from this devotional practice in order to appreciate its mental hindrance in seeing the facts of experience clearly and gauging the trends of the future.
So long as history is regarded as sacred ground, military
science must remain where science as a whole was centuries back. It has not yet emerged from the Middle
Ages. With a general broadening of outlook among
those who are now rising to the higher places of the
Army, there is hope of similar progress at the military
colleges, but the latter is conditioned by the former, and
we cannot expect it to be as fast as is necessary. It might
be quickened if the process of education was moved to
places where the desired atmosphere already prevails.

A suggestion of a different kind, but with the same
aim of making the Army a career attractive to talent,
is the creation of a special Staff Corps. It might be recruited from university graduates who had taken a good
honours degree, forming an intellectual *élite* from which
the higher direction of the Army could in turn be recruited—with the double advantage that they would
have been trained from the outset for the work, and
have escaped years of deadening routine. Such a system
would enable better use to be made of the university
route of entry than at present, without necessarily en-
larging its scale. It would apply to the Army the long-
tested method by which the Civil Service provides its
higher, administrative class. It might be made more elastic by providing opportunity, for subsequent entry into
the Corps, to regimental officers whose gifts had been
late in maturing, or even to Territorial officers of out-

standing military ability who had found, as not infrequently happens, that their natural hobby should have been their chosen profession. The creation of such a Staff Corps would enable permanent rates of pay to be offered sufficient to attract the ablest university products, and to keep them in the service—whereas, to-day, the ablest of the younger staff officers are being tempted to leave the service early by the slowness of promotion and the poorness of the pay in comparison with what men of their age and calibre can command outside.

The obvious danger in forming a separate Staff Corps is that its members might become out of touch with the problems and difficulties of the ordinary soldier, leading to consequent friction and to the issue of unpractical directions. But this danger already exists, and has long made itself felt, in the present system. To-day, perhaps more than ever, the gates of the Staff College control the level of advancement, and its hallmark is a badge of separation. Moreover, nothing is more conducive to friction between the Staff and the Line than the fact that many an aspiring soldier ultimately finds the gates of the Staff College closed to him, and is filled with a bitter sense of having wasted twelve or fifteen years in a profession which now has no future for him. With a Staff Corps recruited direct from the Universities he would have a fair idea of his destiny from the outset, while being able to keep a hope of joining the elect, instead of, as at present, hanging under a fear of eventual disappointment.

To give members of such a Staff Corps an understanding of regimental conditions, and to prevent them losing it, it would certainly be necessary for them to do spells of duty with a unit at intervals throughout their career. Except at the outset this would merely be a continuation of the present system, with the nominal difference that they would be seconded from the staff to a unit, and the beneficial difference that their departure, for return to the staff, would be no cause of grievance to the regiment. They might also gain in experience by doing their spells of regimental duty with different arms, thus becoming better equipped for the direction of combined forces. The drawbacks of a separate Staff Corps are obvious; they tend to diminish, and the advantages to become more manifest, in reflection. Here I must confess that, for my own part, I have hitherto viewed with disfavour anything which might widen the gulf between the Staff and the regimental soldier, having seen so much of the troubles which arise under the present system. Thus when I originally referred to the old, if vague, suggestion for a Staff Corps, I had the half-formed thought that it would suffice to point out the drawbacks; it was only as I continued to think about it, and the possibility of utilizing it as a development of the university entry, that I began to change my view, becoming more impressed by its potential advantages. The ills are already inherent in the existing staff system; a higher extension of that system might lessen them while improving its value—on the principle of cure by "the hair of the dog that bit him".

Whatever the merits of these several suggestions for raising the level of military ability, it is well to realize that it will be a long time before their application can appreciably improve the situation. Even if any of them were adopted forthwith, many years would pass before the officers educated in such a fresh atmosphere would rise to the high places of the Army. During those years they would be affected by the successive layers of their seniors, and be passing on the effects to their juniors. Thus, if they rose to the top in forty years, it would be still too much to expect that in another forty years the atmosphere there would become as clear of traditional dust as their own had been when they left the university eighty years before. To gauge the implications of that time-lag is a check on optimism. Nor is it the only one. We may recognize the value of a university training as a means of broadening the mind, but we should avoid the mistake of overestimating the effect. If it raises a hope, it is by no means a guarantee of freedom from prejudice and the capacity to weigh questions impartially. An hour in some common-rooms would suffice to dispel such illusions. By contrast, some of the broadest minds have passed through the narrowest grooves. The man is more than the system. The best system of education is no more than a help, although a bad one is a hindrance.

Thus, any of the suggested reforms that might be made in the education of officers are, at the most, only hopeful forms of treatment; they are not a solution of the problem—of developing adequate adaptability to the conditions of future warfare. This turns on the simple yet fundamental question of *attitude*. To cope with the problems of modern war we need, above all, to see them clearly and analyze them scientifically. This requires freedom from prejudice combined with the power of discernment and with a sense of proportion. Only through the capacity to see all relevant factors, to weigh them fairly, and to place them in relation to each other, can we hope to reach an accurately balanced judgment. Discernment may be primarily a gift; and a sense of proportion, too. But their development can be assisted by freedom from prejudice, which largely rests with the individual to achieve—and within his power to achieve it. Or at least to approach it. The way of approach is simple, if not easy—requiring, above all, constant self-criticism and care for precise statement.

It is easier, however, to find an index of progress, and consequently of fitness to bear the responsibility of exercising judgment. If a man reads or hears a criticism of anything in which he has an interest, watch whether his first question is as to its fairness and truth. If he reacts to any such criticism with strong emotion; if he bases his complaint on the ground that it is not in "good taste", or that it will have a bad effect—in short, if he shows concern with any question except "Is it true?" he thereby reveals that his own attitude is unscientific. Likewise if in his turn he judges an idea not on its merits but with reference to the author of it; if he criticizes it as "heresy"; if he argues that authority must be right because it is authority; if he takes a particular criticism as a general depreciation; if he confuses opinion with facts; if he claims that any expression of opinion is "unquestionable"; if he declares that something will "never" come about, or is "certain" that any view is right. The path of truth is paved with critical doubt, and lighted by the spirit of objective enquiry. To view any question subjectively is self-blinding. There is nothing more astounding, if amusing, than the way many a soldier, for example, in his heated denunciation of some criticism of soldiers' limitations, will prove out of his own mouth that it is at least correct in his own case. So, to end on a lighter note, I would suggest to my readers that they may learn something by watching how various soldiers, and themselves if soldiers, react to this discussion of the problem of developing the scientific approach to military problems. And if they are not soldiers, they may gain additional profit by observing their own and their fellows' reaction to a critical examination of their own profession.

PART III: FORECASTS

15

The Last War and the Next

IF SOME COUNTRIES ANNOUNCE THEIR SCHEMES of rearmament as a regretful necessity, while others announce it in tones of martial pride, a feature common to all is the air of confidence that the measures are technically sound. They all appear satisfied that the fact of rearmaments is equivalent to efficiency. Is such confidence justified? Past experience hardly supports it, and the doubt is increased by the complexity of the conditions which surround any future war. Any reasonable man must hope that war will have no future: but a reasonable man must know that reason plays small part in human affairs. And experience does not lend much encouragement to the hope of no more war.

"What will the next war be like?" "Will it be anything like the last?" These are questions that, in the present state of apprehension or resigned curiosity, are almost daily hurled at anyone who is a student of the grim branch of knowledge which is sometimes called the science of war. Such a description is far too flattering —the neatest comment upon it that I have seen was one by Rebecca West to the effect that: "Before a war military science seems a real science, like astronomy, but that after a war it seems more like astrology."

Those who have progressed furthest in exploration realize that its scientific study has barely begun. They will also be the least inclined to venture upon detailed predictions. Confident prophecy is best left to generals, who as a class have a traditional fondness for it, and as prophets have no reputation to lose. We have only to recall some of their prophecies that stand on record.

If there was one feature of the half-century preceding 1914 that would seem impossible to misjudge, it was the increasing advantage of the defensive, due to the growing power of infantry firearms—first the magazine rifle and then the machine-gun. An obvious corollary was the limitation placed on cavalry action. The American Civil War, as it advanced, made these new factors plain. It was not to be expected that European generals would profit by this second-hand experience, since the great Von Moltke dismissed it as no more than "two armed mobs chasing each other round the country, from which nothing could be learned". But the Franco-German War, despite its brevity, demonstrated at Gravelotte and elsewhere the same change of conditions. Nevertheless in 1883 we find the German protagonist of the "Nation in Arms", the future Field-Marshal von der Goltz, declaring that "the idea of the greater strength of the defensive is a mere delusion". The Boer War might surely have suggested a doubt of this dictum, yet in 1903 the future Marshal Foch, already acting as the official mould of French military ideas, committed himself to the confident prediction that "any improvement in firearms is bound to strengthen the offensive".

He at least had not been a participant in any real test, but the future Field-Marshal Haig, called upon by the Royal Commission, when fresh from the South African battlefields, to give account of the light that he had gained, was confident that "cavalry will have a larger sphere of action in future wars". His forecast might have been more intelligible if he had been thinking merely of mounted troops, which had been necessary to cope with Boer mobility. But he showed that his mind was fixed on the cavalry charge by the stress he laid on mounted *action,* and he confirmed this subsequently by the severe measures he took to curb the tendency to turn cavalry into mounted riflemen.

His view was shared by the military authorities of all the Continental Powers, with the result that in 1914 Germany, France, Russia, and Austria each deployed over a hundred thousand cavalry. With what result? The French relied for their information mainly on their cavalry, but, as has now been officially related: "This immense mass of cavalry discovered nothing of the enemy's advance . . . and the French Armies were everywhere surprised." The most important effect that the German cavalry achieved was that, by their reckless destruction of telegraph lines everywhere, they did much to paralyze their own command during the advance into France. The Austrians' advance was "preceded by a great mass of cavalry"; their official history records that most of them never came within sight of the enemy, owing to their horses being disabled through sore backs.

They at least were luckier than those who did make contact. For since the Russian cavalry stayed behind, the remaining Austrian cavalry bumped into the Russian infantry; poor shots as these were they did not fail to hit such a target, and the Austrian cavalry came back with nothing to compensate their heavy casualties.

This cavalry prelude was overshadowed by the drama that followed, when the main armies clashed, but it was perhaps the hugest farce that has ever been enacted in a theatre of war.

The generals were no more fortunate in gauging the possibilities of newer instruments. Not many years before 1914, when the attention of a member of the British Army Council was drawn to a note on the development of aircraft, he endorsed it thus: "We are no nearer the solution of the conquest of the air than we were in the days of Montgolfier's Fire Balloon." A more comprehensive disbelief in change was expressed by General Sukhomlinov, the Russian War Minister who warned the instructors at the Staff College that he could "not hear the words 'modern war' without a feeling of annoyance. As war was, so it remains; all these things are vicious innovations." Sukhomlinov was disappointed of his ambition to command the Russian Armies in the war, but he could at least content himself with having helped to ensure that they marched blind and little better than armless to the slaughter.

Different in form, but fundamentally similar in nature, was the assurance of the French Commander-in-Chief, Joffre, when on August 6th, 1914, he serenely declared: "It may be concluded that the Germans are executing a plan of which we have knowledge." Hence it was with ample confidence that he launched his forces eastward into Lorraine, and into a trap, while the Germans were sweeping through Belgium.

If the German Command thus scored an initial surprise, they threw away the advantage through an over-confidence that verged on intoxication. They told the Austrians that if the French Army took the offensive they counted on attaining a decision "on the 21st day of mobilization", i.e. August 23rd. If the French Army stayed on the defensive behind its frontier defence, they might take a week longer to achieve a decisive victory. They would then transfer their forces to the Russian front where they "should arrive on the 41st day of mobilization". The decision had not come when August 22nd came, although that day the French, advancing blindly, ran into the advancing Germans in the Ardennes, and were thrown back. Although mauled, they slipped away. Yet the German Command was sufficiently persuaded that the decisive victory had already been won that, on the 25th, it began transferring forces to Russia from the right wing. By the time this reached the Marne, it was much weaker than the forces opposing it. And on the 41st day of mobilization, September 11th, it was in full retreat!

The decisive turn had come with the penetration of the British Expeditionary Force into a thirty-mile gap between the two German armies of the right wing. This gives an ironical turn to the fact that the German Command had rebuffed the offer of their Navy to interfere with the shipment of the British force, saying that "it would be of advantage to settle with the 160,000 British at the same time as the French and Belgians".

The blindness of generalship, especially towards new developments, was not cured by sharp contact with reality—partly, perhaps, because that contact was at second-hand. The German machine-guns had paralyzed movement on the battlefield for months when Haig, resisting a proposal for increasing the British strength in these weapons, remarked that: "The machine-gun was a much overrated weapon and two per battalion were more than sufficient." Called upon for his judgment, Kitchener conceded that four per battalion might be useful, but anything "above four may be counted a luxury". Long before the war ended, there would be a scale of more than forty heavy and light machine-guns per battalion—but that was due to the foresight and forceful pressure of a civilian minister, Mr. Lloyd George.

Military myopia likewise prevailed when means were mooted to overcome the defensive barrier formed by the hostile machine-guns. When the project of building tanks was submitted to the British Engineer-in-Chief in June, 1915, he icily remarked: "Before considering this proposal we should descend from the realms of imagination to solid facts." Eight months later, when the first tank performed in front of Lord Kitchener, his comment was: "A pretty mechanical toy. The war," he added, "would never be won by such machines."

Most of the generals were confident that it would be won long before such unnecessary aids could be produced. They had been equally confident from the earliest months, and they remained so despite constant disproof.

On September 13th, 1914, General Wilson, the right hand of the British Commander-in-Chief, unwisely noted in his diary a conversation he had had with the guiding brain of the French: "Berthelot asked me when I thought we should cross into Germany, and I replied ... in four weeks. He thought three weeks." That very day the Allied armies were held up on the line of the Aisne, where they remained for the next four years.

The following June, Poincaré, the French President, pathetically complained to Kitchener: "Joffre and Sir John (French) told me in November they were going to push the Germans back over the frontier; they gave me the same assurance in December, March, and May. What have they done? The attacks are very costly and end in nothing."

Lest it might be imagined that these optimistic forecasts were merely, if rashly, uttered to encourage ministerial morale, one must record a few more prophecies in which the generals indulged in their own circle. Thus, in November, 1914, Sir John French asserted that all the hard fighting of the war was over; in January, 1915, he expressed the opinion that the war would be over before June; in February, Joffre said that it would be over by July; in March, Haig felt sure that the Germans would be wanting peace before the end of July; in August, he declared that he would not be surprised to see the enemy give in by November, and that in any case they could not go on after January, 1916.

When it came to preparing the great offensive of July 1st, 1916, Haig and his chief executive, as the British Official History records, "impressed on all, at con-

ferences and other times, that the infantry would only
have to walk over and take possession of" the enemy
trenches. The actual attack on July 1st was a complete
failure on the greater part of the front, with a loss of
60,000 men in a single day.

At the end of 1916, continued disappointment led to
the replacement of Joffre by Nivelle, who planned a
great offensive for 1917, declaring: "We shall break the
German front when we wish." When his executive sub-
ordinate, General Micheler, reported that the enemy
were building a new third line of defence out of reach
of his artillery, Nivelle lightheartedly retored: "Don't
be anxious, you won't find a German in those trenches;
they only want to be off!" He confidently asserted that
he would break through the Germans' first two positions
"with insignificant loss", that in three days at most his
armies would be in open country, beginning the great
pursuit to the Rhine. The offensive was duly launched
and at nightfall had progressed about 600 yards instead
of the six miles anticipated in Nivelle's programme; its
continuation on subsequent days did little more than increase the loss to a total of 120,000. The chief effect was
to strain the morale of the French troops to breaking-
point, producing a dangerous series of mutinies in the
attack-sickened army. It was crippled for the rest of the
summer and had to be nursed carefully for the rest of
the war.

Notwithstanding the paralysis of his allies, Haig told
the British Cabinet in June 1917, that "if the fighting
were kept up at its present intensity for six months Germany would be at the end of her available man-power".

By such assurances he gained a dubious sanction for his own continued offensive at Ypres. On August 21st he reported to the Government that "the time is fast approaching when Germany will be unable to maintain her armies". On October 8th, arguing for permission to press deeper into the Passchendaele morass, he declared that the enemy might collapse "at any moment". With obvious doubt, as if making a concession to pessimistic politicians, he prefaced his view of 1918 prospects with the remark: "Even if they hold out until next year." But even if they did, and were able to transfer troops from the Russian front, he did not contemplate any serious check to his offensive. Not by a single word did he suggest the possibility that the Germans might take the offensive. As late as January 7th, 1918, when he came home to see the Cabinet, he expressed the opinion that the Germans would not attack. But on March 21st, they refuted his prophecy, by breaking through his front to a depth of nearly forty miles.

If the series of crises that followed were retrieved, and the scales of the war turned, by the arrival of American reinforcements, it was the pressure of sea-power that undermined Germany's resistance and ensured her collapse. This fact lends significance to the French Command's pre-war estimate of the help that the British Navy would afford. Colonel Repington, the military critic, had written in *The Times* that it was "worth 500,000 bayonets to the French". General Wilson, the strategic brain of the British War Office, retorted that "Our Navy was not worth 500 bayonets." After consulting the three leading French soldiers, he wrote: "Castelnau and Joffre did not value it at one bayonet . . . Foch is of exactly the same opinion."

This catalogue of misjudgment by the highest professional opinion should serve as a warning for the future. It should be engraved on the walls of every War College. Even if it does not cure the habit of prophecy among military chiefs, it should make us wary of accepting dogmatic assertions, especially where novel developments are concerned. But there is a further lesson. Such a catalogue goes far to show that Rebecca West was right, and that military science is "more like astrology". Perhaps that conclusion is rather hard on astrology.

There is, doubtless, a science of war; but we are a long way from discovering it. Apart from the mere technique of utilizing weapons, what passes for "military science" is hardly more than the interpretation of conventions nurtured by tradition and warped by sentiment, patriotic and professional. Sentiment and science are incompatible, but this truth has yet to be accepted in the military world. Only two years ago Field-Marshal Sir Philip Chetwode, the Commander-in-Chief in India, reminded an audience at the Quetta Staff College of Marshal Saxe's verdict two centuries ago: "Custom and prejudice, confirmed by ignorance, are the usual foundations of the so-called science of war." Sir Philip Chetwode added that this applies still. If his "military testament" should shake the complacency with present knowledge which tends to make any profession a mere profession of knowledge covering unexplored depths, it may prove not the least, indeed the greatest, of the services he has rendered.

But can we expect that any man's words, however forceful, can strike off the fetters forged by centuries of custom, and riveted by human concern for career, as well as by discipline? Few men, even of such calibre, would venture to be so candid until their careers were complete. And then, too often, their confessions will be pushed aside with a shrug of the shoulders, and the slighting comment: "He's only a retired soldier." The time factor dominates war; too appropriately, it rules the profession of arms. There is perhaps none where the dicta of the man in office are accepted with such uncritical deference, or where the termination of an active career brings a quicker descent into careless disregard. Little wonder that many of them are so affected by the sudden transition as to cling pathetically to the trimmings of the past, and so to justify the stage and printed-page caricatures of their class, caricatures which evoke the mirth of audiences blind to the tragedy. Yet a proportion of such men use retirement as opportunity for reflection, and there is much historical evidence to show that from this section has come more accurate prognostication of future warfare than from the reigning occupants of the seats of authority. The philosophic historian may deduce that truth emerges as ambition recedes.

It is not correct to say that the trend of warfare is impossible to gauge—at least of warfare hitherto. Marshal Foch was making an appropriate confession rather than a scientific statement when he declared in 1926: "The military mind always imagines that the next war will be on the same lines as the last. That has never been the case and never will be." One can well understand that in

retrospect the war looked different to him from anything he had ever conceived, or prophesied of it, beforehand. But the conditions that dumbfounded him and his
fellows were only the climax of an evolutionary process
which they could have detected, but did not. Every war
for half a century, since 1861, had made it plainer. Other
minds did perceive them.

M. Bloch, a civilian banker of Warsaw, gave a remarkably accurate diagnosis of their essential elements in his
War of the Future, published on the eve of the twentieth
century, before he had even the data of South Africa and
Manchuria to confirm his deductions. There were also
military minds, if these belonged to bodies not in the
seats of authority, that foresaw the coming stalemate and
pointed out its chain of causation. Captain Mayer, the
French military critic, was provoked by Foch's fiery advocacy of the offensive to predict, only too well, the
siege war that would engulf generals who were dreaming of mobile war without the means of mobility. He was
boycotted for his audacity. So was the eminent military
historian, Lt.-Colonel Grouard, when he turned from the
past to the future, and forecast in 1911 exactly what
would happen if the French Command adopted such a
plan as they did, in 1914. And, as we have seen, the
British military critic, Colonel Repington, had a far
wider grasp than either the French or British General
Staffs of the factors that would influence the issue of the
war.

While the trend of the future in the past could have
been gauged—and was, by those who could study it in
detachment—it has become far more difficult to foresee

the course of the next war. Apart from the immense development of weapons since 1918, so many of the innovations of 1914–18 are still unassimilated. The military
corporation, indeed, is in a state of acute indigestion.

In 1914, the armies marched to the battlefield on foot
as they had done for centuries. The only difference was
that they were taken part of the way by rail, and that
their reserves could be switched from one flank to
another by that same mechanical means. The main effect
of this change was that such large numbers were vomited
on to the roads beyond railheads as to impede their own
manœuvre, while a supplementary effect, due to more
rapid switching, was that an enemy's manœuvre could
be more easily blocked. The war gave a tremendous impetus to the growth of mechanical transport, both road
and roadless. Motor lorries multiplied by the thousand,
but this acceleration of movement only improved the
capacity of supply; it did not markedly affect strategy
since it could not alter the immobility of fighting troops
who had already been driven, by the machine-gun, to
bury themselves in trenches. The possibility of moving
at 30 m.p.h. was of little avail to soldiers who had been
reduced by a tactical obstacle to 0 m.p.h. To resurrect
movement in face of fire, the fire-support of the attackers
was developed by multiplication—of guns—and by addition—of new weapons, the light machine-gun, the
mortar, the grenade, together with gas, smoke, and flame-
projectors. Some of them contributed to defence as
much as to the attack, and none of them succeeded so far
as to revive war of movement.

Eventually the roadless armour-clad machine, known

as the tank, was introduced; this went further than any other means to overcome the machine-gun obstacle, and by German confession proved the most important military factor in the final phase of the war. But the end came, after a gradual withdrawal, before the tank had been developed far enough to produce more than a local acceleration of movement. In the army that retired, and in the armies that followed it up, a mass of motor vehicles were mingled with a greater mass of horsed vehicles. It is a question whether movement as a whole could have been much quicker even if the machine-gun brake had been lifted. Retardation may have averted confusion. On the other fronts—Bulgarian, Turkish, and Austrian— the brake was less effective, with the consequence that the new air weapon found gorgeous targets. And under its blows the retreating armies dissolved in chaos.

The post-war armies are left with this necklace of novelties, now much developed in quantity and quality —so much developed that calculation of the effect, if war should come again, is more difficult than ever. And the force of tradition has led them, at the same time, to keep their old tools. There has been no scientific redesigning of the structure of armies. Modification has come mainly by accretions due to imitation. Not as a reorganization inspired by a sense of proportion and guided by a revaluation. In most of the armies horses are still mingled with motors, unarmoured road-bound vehicles are linked with tanks, the cult of the bayonet is wreathed around the use of automatic firearms and gas. Soldiers may go into action at any pace between 3 m.p.h. and 30, while from overhead they may be attacked at 300 m.p.h. Is it not possible, even probable, that when these differing rates of movement are added together the sum may be zero?

The Navies of 1914 showed a greater advance on the past than the armies. They were also less tested. Battleships and cruisers were the natural heirs of the old wooden ships of the line and frigates, but through steam and armour they had been so transformed that their properties were difficult to gauge owing to the paucity of naval actions since the mechanized age of naval warfare had dawned. With the invention of the torpedo they had been confronted with a new menace, at first projected by the torpedo-boat—to which the destroyer, developed as a counter—became a successor. If the new weapon had a certain likeness to the old fireship, it had much wider possibilities. These were increased by the advent of the submarine, while the movement of fleets suffered a fresh restriction by the development of mines. It was more difficult to estimate the change of conditions because of the controversy that raged round the torpedo. The conflict of enthusiasm and prejudice produced an atmosphere in which scientific study was suffocated—if it was ever possible among a class who were men of action and had never been educated in a scientific way of thought. The natural result was a compromise by which the maintenance of the existing order was mixed with concessions to the new idea.

Detroyers were added to the battle-fleet, but were tied to its protection rather than applied to an offensive role. As for submarines, at the outbreak of war in 1914, Germany had only twenty-eight, and by 1917 little more than a hundred, out of which only about a third were operating at any particular time. Yet, even apart from their deadly action against commerce, the effect of their latent menace to battleships was such that by the summer of 1916 the British naval authorities were agreed that the Grand Fleet must be kept out of their reach. To quote the British Official Naval History they had "so restricted the movements of a fleet of super-Dreadnoughts —each one of which could steam several thousands of miles without refuelling—that the waters opposite one-third of the eastern coastline of Great Britain, and about half of the North Sea, were outside its zone of effective action". The Germans' paucity of submarines led in turn to the self-imprisonment of their fleet when the available submarines were wanted for the new unrestricted campaign against merchant shipping. The farcical result was thus reached that "for the future the two great battle-fleets could but lie inactive, watching one another across a kind of 'No Man's Sea', where attack and defence were concerned only with transport and commerce". This direct action against the supplies upon which Britain depended for her existence, was carried so far that by the following spring she was in sight of collapse before the danger was brought under control—through the introduction of the convoy system—which in turn depended on the additional destroyers provided by America.

This near-fatal menace was created by a comparative handful of submarines, operating under most disadvantageous geographical conditions, and in waters guarded by 3000 destroyers and light craft—odds of 30 to 1 against the submarines.

When these facts are weighed, they seem to impart a somewhat low gravity, and illogically, to the voices of those naval authorities who, ever since the war, have been proclaiming the ineffectiveness of the submarine and the undiminished sovereignty of the battleship.

Moreover, the single menace offered by the submarine has now become a threefold menace—below the surface, above the surface, and on the surface—through the development of aircraft and of high-speed light craft. Battle-fleets may still be safe and supreme well out on the oceans, but their primary strategic purpose is to secure their country's coasts and ports. Although it is important that a country's merchant ships and transports should be able to sail the oceans safely, such safety will not suffice if they are sunk as they approach harbour. It is in the narrow seas and within reach of coasts—where most of the naval battles of history have been decided—that aircraft, light craft and undersea craft have their opportunity. It may be more than an opportunity; a supremacy, indeed—but there are too many incalculables for anyone to gauge this before the test comes.

It is clear that the value of a battle-fleet is now much restricted, while it is by no means clear that the necessity of having one, for powers that need to use the oceans, has in any way diminished. The burden of defence has increased while the security afforded has decreased. Instead of speaking of the "command of the sea", we can only refer to the "conundrum of the sea".

The evolution of war at sea, as on land, has been towards multiplicity of means and complexity of methods. Simplification is not yet in sight. Moreover, the complexity is augmented by the increasing dependence of the fighting forces upon industrial resources. As a consequence, all the countries are developing schemes of economic mobilization, as a necessary foundation for their military, naval, and aerial mobilization. But this economic mobilization introduces numberless new factors that complicate strategic plans, while it is liable to dislocation by the new types of military pressure that are simultaneously evolving—especially that of air attack. Are the problems of future warfare becoming too complex for solution, at any rate by strategists who have been professionally trained to prefer simple solutions and traditionally nurtured in a preference for familiar means?

Reflection on these conditions suggests that there is only one safe prophecy about the next war—or that the safest prophecy is—that it will prove a greater muddle than the last. That it will begin in confusion and end in chaos. It is not that generals and admirals are incompetent, but that the task has passed beyond their competence. Their limitations are due not to a congenital stupidity—as a disillusioned public is so apt to assume— but to the growth of science, which has upset the foundations of their technique. They are like men who cling to their little wooden huts in an earthquake. The only way of salvation would be to get out in the open— to survey the problems in complete detachment and from the widest point of view,

But a scientific habit of thought is the last thing that military education and training have fostered. Perhaps that is an unalterable condition, for the services might hardly survive if they parted company with sentiment—

if the bulk of their members detached themselves from the loyalties which are incompatible with the single-minded loyalty to truth that science demands.

16

A German View of the Next War

THE DIRECTOR OF GERMANY'S MILITARY EF-
fort in the last war, General Ludendorff, has recently set
forth his ideas on future warfare, and his creed of national life in preparation for it. He seeks to expound the
doctrine of "totalitarian warfare" which should be the
natural accompaniment of the Totalitarian State. Ad-
dressed to his countrymen, his message deserves attention
by other peoples. It also requires examination by scientific students of war.

He opens with a heavy attack on the theories of
Clausewitz which, as he emphasizes, were the foundation
on which the German plans in 1914 had been built.
Clausewitz, who had died nearly a century before,
moulded the minds of the leading soldiers and statesmen,
not only in Germany but throughout Europe, during the
generations which led up to the World War. Since then
his theories have suffered some searching criticism, especially from Anglo-Saxon analysts, for their tendency to
make policy the servant of strategy, and strategy little
more than a strait lane to battle. The theoretical ex-
travagance of Clausewitz's idea of "absolute war"—"vio-

lence pushed to its utmost bounds"—was contrary to common sense. To use force without limit and without calculation of cost may be instinctive in a hate-maddened mob, but it is the negation of statesmanship. Germany's exhaustion in 1918 was the natural consequence of this delusion. The conductors of her war-machine, less wise than Bismarck, did not know when to stop; they went on until they tumbled into the abyss.

Although cause and effect here seem so clear, Ludendorff is still unable to see it. Through his coloured glasses the fault of Clausewitz's teaching is not that it lent itself to such extremes, but that it did not go far enough. It allowed policy too much importance, not too little. As typical of Clausewitz he cites a passage concluding: "The political goal is the end, and warfare is a means leading to it, and means can never be thought of without a certain end." To Ludendorff this is old-fashioned nonsense. The totalitarian principle demands that in war a nation should place everything in its service; and, in peace, at the service of the next war. War is the highest expression of the national "will to give", and politics must therefore be subservient to the conduct of war.

It becomes clear that the main difference between Clausewitz and his successor is that the latter achieves what seemed unthinkable to the former, and "thinks" of war as a means without an end—unless making the nation into an efficient army be considered an end in itself. This is hardly so new as Ludendorff appears to imagine. Sparta tried it, and the end of her existence lies two thousand years back.

With the aim of developing the nation for war, of

creating a super-Sparta, Ludendorff's first concern is to
ensure "the psychical unity of the people". For him "the
Christian faith, and the life shaped by it, are the prime
causes of a national breakdown in the totalitarian war".
This faith must be replaced by one "built on racial con-
victions, where life is rooted in an affined knowledge of
God peculiar to itself": to put it in simpler words—a belief in a purely German God. From this will spring a
healthy nationalism in which all women will accept that
their noblest task is to bear vigorous sons to "bear the
burden of the totalitarian war", and all men will develop
their powers for that purpose: in short—to breed, and be
bred, for killing. The other positive suggestions which
Ludendorff offers towards this problem of creating psychical unity boil down to little more than the age-old
prescription of suppressing everyone who expresses, or
even entertains, views contrary to those of the High
Command.

The next need insisted on is for a sound and self-
sufficient national economic system suited to the demands
of totalitarian war. Ludendorff thus seems to realize that
military power rests on an economic foundation. Yet,
curiously, when he dwells on the crippling difficulties
suffered in the last war, and gives striking evidence of
the effect of the Allied blockade, he does not see how
this reflects on his belief that wars are decided by battle
between the armies. For the only point of praise which
he can give Clausewitz is that "Clausewitz only thinks of
the annihilation of the hostile armies in battle". To
Ludendorff this remains "an immutable principle", although it is a theory which has rarely been borne out in

practice during the century since Clausewitz died. Happily for Ludendorff he is not troubled by historical facts when they present obstacles to his faith.

Let us now study his picture of the way that the totalitarian war will be waged. It should open without a declaration of war—lest the people of the nation which declares war should feel any guilty sense of being the aggressors. Within a few hours of the decision to make war, air, land and sea striking forces must reach their full war readiness. The rest of the air force and navy will complete their mobilization by the second day; and the rest of the land forces, a few days later. Hostilities will have already begun with the despatch of the mechanized divisions near the frontier to force an entry into the enemy country. On the seas the surface and submarine attack on the enemy's commerce will coincide with this opening stroke. "The focussing point of the war now lies in sending air formations to gain air superiority over the enemy, to strike at the advance of the enemy's army by rail and otherwise, and also at aerodromes. Air battles will ensue." It may be worth while also to bomb important industrial towns. Within forty-eight hours or less, the navy should sail to seek decisive battle with the foe. "The main land advance" may begin a little later, because of the masses that will have to be brought up—and these will have to come by rail since motors will be inadequate to carry the numbers. "There is no doubt that by the end of the second week of war, operations will be in full progress everywhere." Battle will follow battle till the enemy is finally crushed, or till reserves of men and material run out. "In the wars waged by continental

countries the decision lies on land." The air force must
first be used to help in beating the opposing army; only
then will the army be able to act "with its air force"
against the enemy country in the rear.

Land, air and sea action all have in common the fight
to bring about a superiority of fire over the enemy.
Nevertheless this will not suffice "to bring about the annihilation of the enemy". "The final decision on land will
lie in the fight of man against man, tank against man, or
tank against tank"—how a tank can destroy a tank, any
more than a warship can destroy a warship, except by
fire, Ludendorff does not explain. For him, the land battle is still a process in which the infantry is helped forward by artillery, machine-guns, mortar and tank support
until it "overwhelms the enemy in a man-to-man fight".
Furthermore, "attack is always the deciding factor in
battles". Army battles with army, supported by aircraft;
navy battles with navy, supported by aircraft; and "in
air battles air squadrons fight one another". All movements should lead to battle; mechanization simply
quickens the rush to battle.

Ludendorff has no moral objection to striking direct
against the enemy people. "The demands of totalitarian
warfare . . . will ever ignore the cheap theoretical desire
to abolish unrestricted U-boat warfare." And aircraft
will now combine with submarines in sinking every ves-
sel which tries to reach the enemy's ports, "even vessels
sailing under neutral flags". Likewise on land a time will
come "when bombing squadrons must inexorably and
without pity be sent against" the people in the enemy
country. But on military grounds, which are the ruling

considerations, that time should normally be delayed until the battles have been won.

Ludendorff declares that technical means are becoming ever more important, yet clings to the old belief that strength lies in numbers—"it is a fact that 'victory goes to the big battalions'." Hence "the totalitarian war demands the incorporation in the Army of every man fit to bear arms". He admits that the conditions of war require the fighting man to be increasingly individualistic, yet assumes that this is compatible with the strictest discipline, and fails to reflect that the Totalitarian State is hardly the soil in which such individualism can flourish. He has a welcome for every new weapon and instrument, but rarely appears to consider how they may affect each other. He conveys no clear picture, and seems to have none himself, of the different factors of war in relation to each other. His message would seem to be—multiply every kind of force as much as you can, and you will get somewhere—but where, he neither worries nor wonders. The one thing on which he is really clear is that "the Commander-in-Chief must lay down his instructions for the political leaders, and the latter must follow and fulfil them in the service of warfare".

What is offered in return for this claim to unlimited power for the military chief, this demand for a blank cheque on the resources of the nation? A faith, certainly —if it requires limitless faith to swallow it. The main articles of Ludendorff's creed might be phrased thus: "I believe in a pure German God, the maker of the German nation in arms; and in the Commander-in-Chief, his only son and representative on earth. I believe in the almighty power of numbers; in battle, as the means to winning war; in attack, as the means of winning battle; and in the hand-to-hand fight as the ultimate means of overcoming the enemy's resistance."

While it is clear that Ludendorff's faith is built on the traditional military theory, despite his sweeping repudiation of the theorists, and that it is essentially derived from the past, it is difficult to find solid support for it even in past experience. It is easier to find the wars where battle did not prove decisive than where it did. Take the first great war of modern history—the Thirty Years' War. There were many battles in which one army was virtually destroyed, yet none had any decisive influence on the struggle. The mutual exhaustion had such effect, however, and made so deep an impression on military thought, that for nearly two centuries the average general was chary of fighting battles at all, while even the great ones took care only to fight when, by chance or by strategy, the dice were loaded heavily in their favour—when, as Saxe said, there was "all imaginable reason to expect the victory . . . without trusting anything to accident".

There was a change when Napoleon came on the scene. A Corsican, not a Frenchman; a supreme careerist, not a true patriot; he was unchecked in pursuing his ambitions by any sense of responsibility for the ultimate welfare of his country as apart from himself. If his dreams were boundless, he took short views, since his horizon was his own life-span. Time was always against him; and he needed quick results. Now, whatever be the difficulties of winning a war by a battle, it is the quickest means—*if* it can be achieved. Hence Napoleon's predisposition for this means.

In adopting it, too, he was helped by new assets. First was the newly introduced organization of the army in independent divisions—whereby, instead of being a single body, it grew limbs—with which it could grip the enemy at one point while it struck him elsewhere. This made it easier to force a battle on the enemy, to take him at a disadvantage, and to concentrate strength against weakness—while hindering the enemy's concentration. Another asset was the new mobility. The revolutionary armies could no longer maintain, or be maintained by, the old elaborate supply system. They had to find a new and flexible system; they had to secure their supplies where they could; they had to learn to live sparsely and march light. The troops themselves could not be kept in the old stiff-drilled formations, nor restrained to a slow pace for the sake of symmetry. But they could cover the country much faster than their opponents, and made rings round them on the battlefield. A further asset was the new artillery method—of concentrating fire rapidly against key-points; of disorganizing the resistance by this blasting fire before the assault was launched.

But even in Napoleon's hands, unlimited battle ultimately proved an unlimited liability. The military splendour of the Napoleonic age fixed the worship of battle like a yoke round the neck of soldiers. Yet the later Napoleonic wars were not decided by battles. Napoleon destroyed the Spanish armies only to find his trouble beginning. And it was not by battles that the Spanish guerillas undermined his power in Spain, and started his general ruin. Napoleon beat the Russian armies, but he did not beat Russia. The Russians wrecked his army by avoiding battle until Generals Hunger and Winter could get to work, and his real downfall was consummated in 1814—when the Allies sealed his fate by swooping on Paris while he was trying to tempt them to meet him in battle.

The American Civil War saw plenty of battles—and Lee's failure to win a victory at Gettysburg certainly damped the hopes of the South. But it was Sherman's back door entry into the South, his strategic march through Georgia and the Carolinas, which undermined the will of the Confederacy by an attack on their supplies and the morale of the people.

The last war was filled with battles, yet the most that the historian can fairly say is that they were a contributory factor—one of many—the main factor in the collapse of Germany being economic pressure. On this point there is Haig's own confession, at the end of October, 1918: "Germany is not broken in a military sense. During the last weeks her armies have withdrawn . . . in excellent order." The Allied armies were exhausted and needed to be reorganized before they could follow up. But Germany was broken internally by hunger, sickness and despair. Her breakdown developed directly from military disappointment, from the depression which spread when her own offensive in the spring failed to bring the victory that Ludendorff had promised. But the foundations of her resistance had been undermined by the Allied blockade.

The abortiveness of battle as a means of winning wars

can be traced to the declining power of the attack to overcome defence. This condition was due to the growing power of modern firearms, and had been long in evolution. It was first manifest in the American Civil War, where it came to be a standard calculation that one man in a trench was equal to three or four in an assault. In Europe the wars of 1866 and 1870 brought fresh evidence of the paralyzing influence of fire, although the brevity of both wars tended to obscure it. Nevertheless, after the second, the winning strategist of those two wars, Moltke, drew the conclusion that his victory could not be repeated, and enunciated the lesson that: "As a result of the improvement of firearms, the tactical defensive has acquired a great advantage over the offensive. . . . It seems to be more advantageous to proceed to an attack only after having repelled several attacks by the enemy." His warning was lost on his successors. Their optimistic view, as expressed by von der Goltz, was: "The idea of the greater strength of the defence is a mere delusion." The optimism was shared in France where, near the end of the century, the future Marshal Foch coined the axiom that "any improvement in firearms is bound to strengthen the offensive"—and proved it to his own satisfaction by specious arithmetic. British experience in the war against the Boers showed the fallacy of such assumptions, but was merely regarded in Europe as evidence of the frailty of the British attacks. Then came the Russo-Japanese war which foreshadowed nearly all the factors which upset military calculations in 1914—the paralyzing power of machine-guns, the hopelessness of frontal attacks, and the consequent re-

lapse of the armies into trenches. But military optimism
was even more impregnable—to the assault of facts. To
ardent soldiers war was unthinkable without successful
attack, so that they were able to persuade themselves
that attacks could succeed. The delusive basis of that
faith was quickly exposed when the World War began,
and was made clearer still when the trench deadlock set
in—for four years. And it is significant that the only
great battles which had far-reaching results before
morale had broken down were those which took the
form of a counter-stroke after the enemy had spent himself in vain attacks—the Allied victories in the first and
second battles of the Marne, the German victories at
Tannenberg, Gorlice, and Caporetto. Yet none of the
commanders at the outset, and hardly any later, showed
remembrance of Moltke's advice, or were willing to delay their own offensive dreams until they had dispelled
the enemy's.

The historical basis of the belief in the hand-to-hand
fight is equally false, and it reacts on the belief in numbers. For a century the military manuals of Europe had
continued to emphasize the decisive importance of physical shock, echoing Clausewitz's dictum: "The close
combat, man to man, is plainly to be regarded as the real
basis of combat." The French doctrine of 1914 fervently
declared that the object of all attacks was "to charge the
enemy with the bayonet in order to destroy him." (That
idea would still remain in the British manuals until 1924.)
Something might be claimed for it if the emphasis had
been on the psychological effect of a close-quarter threat,
but the time and attention devoted to bayonet-training

showed that the bayonet-fight was regarded as a reality. Yet even in the eighteenth century a practical soldier like Guibert had remarked its rarity, while Jomini was but one of a number of witnesses of the Napoleonic battles who said that, except in villages and defiles, he had "never seen two forces cross bayonets". Half a century later Moltke would point out the fallacy of the French assertion that their victory at Solferino had been won by the bayonet. In 1870 their troops were to pay heavily against Prussian fire for this delusion among their leaders, yet Boguslawski records that in actual fact "bayonets were never crossed in open fight".

Only in conditions where shock was a practical possibility could the theory of massing superior numbers be effective. It was difficult to adjust it to conditions where one man with a machine-gun might count for more than a much larger number who were advancing upon him with the bayonet. As the capacity to make such an adjustment proved to be lacking, the formula of victory became merely a formula of futility—and death. The fallacy was proved most emphatically of all by the Germans against the Russians; by their superior weapons and technique the Germans utterly discounted the vastly superior numbers of their Eastern front opponent. There the "big battalions" merely made big cemeteries, burdened their own communications to breaking point, and bankrupted their own country's power, yet the lesson is largely lost on the man who directed the German forces. After twenty years for reflection he resuscitates these delusions for application in another war.

Nevertheless we should be unwise to ignore them, and

to accept instead the popular assumption that the next war will be waged in the air with the contending powers each seeking to destroy the enemy's capital and bomb the people into surrender.

It is worth while to approach the problem of future warfare along Ludendorff's path, not because his idea of the result is likely to prove real, but because it shows what is likely to be attempted. It is a guide to the outlook which still prevails among many of the military chiefs of Europe, to the persistence of obsolete conceptions along with new weapons, and to the consequent confusion of military thought. The general trend of the rearmament race now in progress fosters this by piling up numbers and by feeding the military chiefs with more means than their minds can assimilate. Ludendorff's is a fair representation of what may occur at the outset, if not in the issue, of a future war.

Mechanization has given the general staffs a new ground for belief in mobile warfare—the picture to which armies always revert in peace-time—along with a renewed confidence in the speedy success of their own attacks. Prolonged as was the resistance which the military authorities everywhere offered to the idea of mechanization, now that they have embraced it they build expectations on it which dumbfound a sober and long-standing advocate of this inevitable evolution. In many countries they have burst out into prophecy that trench-warfare is a thing of the past, and that the wars of the future will be fought and finished with a quickness hitherto unknown.

For the initial movements mechanized troops certainly

offer a great advantage over those who have to march on foot or be brought forward by rail. This is the more important because of the growth of new fortifications along the frontiers; the prospects of an invasion will obviously be handicapped if the enemy is given time to man these with the reserves that become available on mobilization. Thus there is little doubt that the new mechanized divisions which the European armies now possess will be used in the first hours of war with the aim of penetrating the enemy's frontier and opening the way for the subsequent general advance. All the general staffs are trending towards this new picture, in which the first phases of a war are fought out by the mechanized part of their forces actually available, instead of waiting, as in 1914, until the main strength of the army has been assembled.

But there is reason to doubt whether this mechanized spearhead will produce the decisive advantage which is sought. The chances are against this, unless the enemy is not only taken unaware but is himself unmechanized. For, in the first place, obstruction is the natural antidote to the power of delivering mobile strokes which mechanization has revived. By utilizing rivers, canals, and railways as barriers, by demolishing bridges and blocking defiles, the defender may go far to nullify the new menace. Moreover, mechanization itself enables the means of obstruction and demolition to be moved more swiftly to any threatened spot. And the defenders' mechanized troops, having less risk of being checked by hostile obstructions, may be switched to meet the danger faster than the mechanized attackers can develop it.

Despite the apparent advantage that mechanization has brought to the offensive, its reinforcement of the defensive may prove greater still.

While the prospects of this initial stroke by the mechanized forces are slight, they are bright compared with those that await the main masses of the European armies. Even if these come close enough to strike, what ground is there for expecting that they will make more impression on the defence than in the last war? The main weapon that then stopped them was the machine-gun: there is now a far higher proportion of machine-guns, light and heavy, in all armies. The weapon on which the attackers mainly relied to overcome the defending machine-gun in the last war was artillery: there is far less artillery now in all armies than in 1918. Even if this could be increased to the wartime scale, it is a weapon that, when used in mass, tends to block the path of the infantry it is trying to help by ploughing up the ground. It acts as an automatic military brake. Furthermore, it increases the encumbrance by the mass of transport required to supply its heavy appetite for shells. Armour, in the form of the tank, proved a better means in the last war of helping the attack forward: but armour used in a direct assault against organized defence would now seem to have lost much of its value, through the great and widespread development of armour-piercing weapons— there are now highly efficient anti-tank machine-guns, and even rifles, as well as guns.

There are greater possibilities, as I have elsewhere suggested, in the skilful use of obscurity as a cloak to the attack. Fog, natural or artificial, and darkness are the best antidotes to the defensive machine-gun. The risks of obscurity are mainly those of confusion; they are certainly less than those of annihilation, by machine-guns with a clear field of fire; and they can be much reduced by training. The superiority of highly trained troops over normal troops is much more pronounced in the dark than in daylight. Such a level of training, however, is difficult to attain during peace-time in mass armies raised by conscription.

But the greater question that affects these mass armies is whether they will ever reach the battlefield. Their approach must be made by roads and railways; they will crowd these arteries which now, for several hundred miles back, lie under the menace of air attack. Their immense demands in food and ammunition supply require a continuous circulation along these arteries; thus the strain and the susceptibility to interruption are maintained all the way back even when the armies themselves have passed on. To gauge what might happen it is worth studying the process of mobilization and assembly in 1914. Despite all the care and effort devoted to its machinery there were hitches which caused serious trouble, and threatened worse. Yet in 1914 there was no interference from the enemy such as is certain to-day through the intervention of air-power—from bombs on the bridges and rail junctions as well as on the trains and marching columns themselves; probably also from mustard gas sprayed over the roads, stations, bivouacs, and supply depots. There is no need to assume that the devastation will be as overwhelming as popular imagination and air enthusiasm picture. The complexity and delicacy of the process of mobilizing and moving forward an army is such that a mere touch, or series of touches, may well suffice to cause its collapse. The larger the army, and the more its mobilization process is speeded up, the more susceptible it will be to dislocation, because the greater will be the congestion of all the traffic arteries.

If the opponent should employ mustard gas, the paralysis of war is still more probable, for in the fighting zone mustard gas is most effective as a defensive blocking agent; it constitutes the most impassable, if invisible, barrier to advance, especially advance by armies composed of infantry; while in the rear zone it is essentially a dislocating agent, upsetting administrative arrangements and traffic circulation. But mustard gas is not essential to produce this stagnation. Machine-guns and demolitions should suffice to stop an advancing army; air bombs acting on inherent congestion behind should suffice to prevent its remaining where it has stopped. Blocked in front, the mass army is likely to break down in rear. If the maintenance of such armies is straining the resources of the nations in peace, in war the attempt to use them threatens national bankruptcy.

The attempt to seek victory in battle at sea has hardly more promise. Here again there is no need to imagine that the battle-fleets will be bombed to destruction. If the battle-fleets of the last war were deterred from meeting each other by the menace of the submarine and the mine, how much more likely is such a paralyzing effect now that to these weapons are added the new dangers introduced by shore-based aircraft and torpedo-carrying speedboats—the little "sea-sleds" which are fast multiplying in many navies.

As for battle in the air, here at present is a sphere where the offensive is superior to the defensive. But that offensive need not take the form of striking at the hostile air forces; it is simpler, far simpler, than it has ever been on land, to strike direct at the sources of the enemy's power without first breaking through his shielding forces. The spaces of the air are so vast and the speeds of aircraft are becoming so high that it is a waste of effort to fight when it is possible to slip past. Faithful to military tradition, some of the air forces, especially when under the control of conventional soldiers, may set out to defeat their aerial opponents; but, if so, they stand to lose the war while they are pursuing the battle.

For, coincidently and subsequently, economic pressure will be in progress in all its varied forms—as even Ludendorff foresees. With the growth of social and industrial organization, economic targets have proportionately outgrown military targets, and they have become more sensitive as the latter have become less vulnerable. The complex web of a nation's commerce and industry, its administration and supply, can be easily torn. Externally the flow of its supplies can be more easily reduced to stagnation now that its trade routes are exposed to attack from shore-based aircraft and other new agents of interference.

Military wisdom now lies, not in amassing armies, but in diminishing national vulnerability. This is a compound of factors. The very industry that augments a nation's strength for military action may produce a counter-balancing degree of vulnerability. And the centralization of industry may counteract the growth of industry from a military point of view. Every means of reducing and dispersing targets, and also of decreasing their sensitiveness, should be studied and sought. The preparedness of the people is no less important. As safeguards against air attack, for example, education and understanding count at least as much as concrete measures for the provision of anti-aircraft weapons and shelters. A sturdy individualism based on a regime of reason and freedom, so long as it does not relapse into inertia, may withstand the shocks better than the emotionalism bred by totalitarianism, with its insistence on mass psychology and incessant appeal to mass sentiment. The self-reliant individual, capable of thinking for himself, has a better chance of adaptation to the unexpected. And the one certainty about modern war is that it is more uncertain than it ever was.

Compared with to-day, it was simple to make military calculations in 1914; yet nearly all the calculations went astray—and the favourite failed. To launch a war nowadays, as remarked in an earlier chapter, is like backing a horse that has never run, and whose breeding even is unknown. If calculation ruled the rulers, they would surely abstain from aggression. But ambitious and warlike rulers are apt to prove the most hardened of gamblers. Napoelon is their patron saint—and there never was a worse case of obstinate self-delusion than his triumphal assurance on the march to Moscow. His kind may still produce gamblers of that kind. But they carry their own antidote so long as they concentrate on building armies for battle, and thereby burden their war organization with a weight it can no longer safely bear. There might be more reason to fear them if they were to develop a new art of war aiming at paralysis rather than annihilation, and operating by multiple pressure without combat: a super-guerilla warfare aimed at the sources instead of at the face of the enemy's armed power, and striking at the greatest number of points—economic, political and psychological—over the widest area, without offering a target or coming to a clinch.

17

The Abyssinian War — and Its Bearing on Future Warfare

THE MAIN LESSONS OF THIS WAR, AS NOW clarified by post-war evidence from both sides, have been briefly discussed in Chapter 3; also their bearing on the question of future warfare. The course of the war did not run according to common expectation, and the situation after the first three months of war encouraged such excessive confidence in the Abyssinians' capacity for resistance that the dramatically swift ending of the main campaign tended to magnify the impression of surprise in the public mind. The Italians themselves have admitted that they had not foreseen the plight in which they found themselves at the end of 1935, nor such rapid and extensive success as ultimately crowned their efforts. Yet it was a war where the determining factors and conditions worked out, on the whole, in a way remarkably true to their calculable properties. That fact is an encouragement to those who believe that there is value in applying what is called the scientific method to the study of war, and that by its use it should be possible to gauge the general current and the local eddies with reasonable accuracy—instead of seeing their effects as the sport of accident and opportunism, and submitting fatalistically to the opinion that every new war must find us unprepared for its conditions.

If the study of war in the past has so often proved fallible as a guide to the course and conduct of the next war, it does not imply that war is not suited to scientific study, but that the study has not been scientific enough, in spirit and method. Looking back on the past it would seem hardly possible that the authoritative schools of military thought could have misunderstood as completely as they did the evolution which was so consistently revealed throughout the wars of the nineteenth and early twentieth centuries. Reviewing the record of error it seems only capable of explanation by the conclusion that their study of war was subjective, not objective—that they went to military history to find texts for their sermons, instead of facts for analysis. That conclusion has been strengthened by experience in trying to estimate the probable course of the Abyssinian War. Here the conditions were so peculiar, and the unknown factors so numerous, that few students could hope to treat the problem with the measure of apparently assured knowledge that was available in recent European wars. It remained to be seen how far the margin of error could be minimized by examining the coming war purely as a problem, without preconceptions and preferences, guided only by a general understanding of recent trends in the evolution of warfare. For my own part I had to attempt such an estimate in the early summer of 1935, and it may be of interest because of the bearing on the question just discussed, to reproduce the bulk of it, as it appeared in *The Times,* before passing on to discuss what actually happened. The retrospective view can thus be compared with the prospective.

PROSPECT

"From a military point of view, the Abyssinian problem may be focussed in a single word: 'Adowa'. Perhaps more exactly, in a phrase: 'The memory of Adowa.' I do not refer here to the part played by the memory of this thirty-nine-year-old defeat in fomenting Italian irritation and increasing determination to attain results that will wipe out the memory. That factor lies in the political sphere, even though it may find expression in the military.

"The military bearing of 'Adowa' lies mainly in its effect upon the attitude and action of the Abyssinians. If it came to a test, would they prove to be intoxicated by that memory of victory over the Italian forces, and imagine that 1896 could be repeated in the conditions of 1935? Would they, in that intoxication, fail to realize that their best hope of successful resistance lies in playing the guerilla game steadfastly from the outset?

"The Abyssinians' most serious danger lies in the possibility that they would, in false confidence, or under the sting of a loss of territory, assemble in mass to oppose the invaders near the frontier. In that case they would offer a promising target to the bombs of the Italian aircraft, and in some areas to the thrusts of mechanized forces. They might even be tempted into launching attacks in vain gallantry against the Italian machine-guns. Omdurman might be repeated. The student of military history appreciates how easily, with a little cunning, the Sudanese might have made things awkward for us in the advance to Khartoum. Instead, by excess of courage they played into our hands, and, by their massed advance in daylight, offered themselves up as a sacrificial demonstration of the effect of fire-power. At the worst, more tactical sense is to be expected of the Abyssinians—but fire-power has developed more in the past thirty years than any improvement in tactics can overtake. The only chance for the ill-equipped nowadays lies in guerilla tactics. Information from some sources makes it doubtful whether the Abyssinians have realized this essential truth, and are of a mind to act upon it. Adowa may prove stronger than reason.

"If the Abyssinians should be so unwise as to present a target to modern weapons, the consequences of a crushing disillusionment are not easy to predict. Its ripples might spread wide. When considering the possible effect of concentrated air bombing on such an unacclimatized people, one recalls the reaction which the Arabs suffered, on the other side of the Red Sea, when they first made contact with artillery fire during the Revolt in the Hejaz against the Turks. The shells which exploded among them were nothing compared with the weight of explosive that the Italian aircraft could drop upon the Abyssinians to-day.

"The Japanese have shown in Manchuria how air bombardment may pave the way for the advancing troops, serving as a longer range and more flexible sub-

stitute for the artillery barrage of the last war. It is likely
that this method will be the Italians' strongest card, with
tanks as a secondary agent, in forcing the evacuation of
points where a prolonged delay might otherwise be imposed. But the further the advance progresses and the
less the defenders offer a target, the greater the handicap
in obtaining the full effect of these new tools.

"If the Abyssinians were wise enough to adopt guerilla
methods from the outset, one does not envy the Italian
commanders the problem that they would be called on
to solve, especially if they aimed at the complete sub-
jugation of the country—and such a country, topograph-
ically. The rugged plateau with its towering escarpment
might be likened to the medieval castle of a giant's
dream. Approaches are few and difficult, being fortified
by nature with successive moats and barricades, while
the communications of an advancing force would be as
hard to safeguard as to create. 'Air-pressure' on the defender's keep would not offer the promise of effect that
this new form of the rear-attack holds out in other parts
of the world, even in similarly de-centralized and unin-
dustrialized states. Addis Ababa, the capital, is over four
hundred miles distant from the Italian bases in Eritrea
and stands over 8000 feet above sea-level; as a bombing
target it would thus seem to be well out of reach of present service aircraft. The air problem might be diminished
as the Italian land forces advance more deeply into the
country—but the further they go the harder may become their military problems. The effective subjuga-
tion of a country largely depends on having targets that
can be effectively smitten. Here, targets will be few un-

less the Abyssinians carelessly offer them. And nothing is more nerve-racking for an army of occupation than the intangible ubiquity of a guerilla foe who is operating in his own country with room enough to play that game.

"But it is far more difficult to change to guerilla methods after a shattering reverse. Here is the risk that the Abyssinians run in remembering Adowa too well. It is true that the Spaniards succeeded in making such a change against the Napoleonic armies, after their own regular forces had been smashed. But they had Wellington to support them and, by his intervention, gained time and space for their guerillas to sprout throughout the country-side. And that successful change of method was achieved more than a century ago; nowadays, air-power and mechanization tend to accelerate the exploitation of victory over a congregated force, and jeopardize the chances of rallying the survivors to harass, where they cannot directly resist, the invaders' progress. Moreover, the nerve-shock of a new weapon is apt to have the deepest echo among a primitive people.

"Such knowledge as we have of the forces and equipment of the Abyssinians strengthens the impression that it would be foolish for them to embark upon an imitation of modern warfare. The number of 'regular' troops of whom the Emperor might dispose are not likely to amount to more than forty thousand, and although levies amounting to more than half a million might be available to oppose an invasion that threatened the heart of the country, such quantities would have little value except for guerilla warfare, even if the miracle of keeping them supplied could be performed. The modern Abyssinian artillery is said to include only some three batteries of '75's'. Beyond this, it is made up of a number of 'elephant-guns' and a hundred or more ancient pieces. Mortars, light aircraft and tanks, may be counted on the fingers. Machine-guns probably total about three hundred, with double that number of automatic rifles—the Arab Revolt showed the essential value of these for guerilla warfare even, and an increase is certainly one of the Abyssinians' most urgent needs, together with adequate ammunition.

"The time the Ethiopians have had for training may not prove altogether an advantage, if one may take as having any general application some recent reports as to the well-drilled state of these troops. That type of training runs the risk of paralyzing their natural fighting instincts and leaving them a paralyzed target. Primitive man knows how to fight with cunning, but if you put him through a long course of drill one may do no more than develop 'tactical arthritis'. To counter the modern weapons of their assailants the Ethiopians do not need similar heavy weapons, any more than they need European drill, but they certainly require an adequate quantity of light machine-guns and small-arm ammunition. These are the material foundation of guerilla tactics against a modern army, as Lawrence of Arabia diagnosed and demonstrated a generation ago on the other side of the Red Sea.

"By contrast, we may reckon that modern armament will give to the Italian troops a fighting value much greater than their actual numbers. The extent of these is not certain, but a short time ago it was reported that there was one white division in Eritrea, with the equivalent of three native divisions, and another white division in Somalia together with a native division. It is probable that about a hundred thousand men have been despatched from the Mediterranean, and although the shipments have dwindled recently, during the bad season, it is likely that the numbers would be increased before operations open. A division in Sardinia has been standing by for some time. The Italian forces are said to include a considerable quantity of tanks and mechanized transport, as well as several hundred aircraft.

"In estimating the possible courses which the Italian forces may adopt, much depends on their object. If they are aiming at the conquest of Abyssinia, the decisive invasion would, in normal expectation, be made from Eritrea. In this case, a main advance from Massawa southward upon Magdala, to bring the Abyssinians to battle, might be accompanied by a flank advance from the southern corner of Eritrea upon the rear of the defending forces. If there is no base in this corner capable of maintaining large forces, the route itself is more suitable to the movement of mechanized troops than along the difficult direct route of advance through the precipitous country between Massawa and Magdala.

"This combined advance from Eritrea might well be preceded by a further advance on the southern borders of Abyssinia, executed by the Italian forces in Somalia. It would serve to draw off the Abyssinians' attention and forces, especially if the threat went far enough and was direct against Harar, the Emperor's own province."

The kernel of my "appreciation" was packed into a nutshell by a Canadian caption-writer who put these headlines on an interview I gave his newspaper on September 4th:

"ADOWA ILLUSION MAY DECIDE WAR SAYS STRATEGIST

Mass Attacks Will Mean Annihilation for Abyssinians Liddell Hart Predicts."

In that interview I also suggested that the Italians might find scope for their aircraft, apart from the normal military functions, in supplying their advanced columns as well as in a progressive demoralization of the population behind the enemy's front.

RETROSPECT

The invasion began on October 2nd. The main Italian forces, three army corps, moved southwards from Eritrea as expected. On the 6th after a short advance they captured Adowa without meeting serious opposition. The Ethiopians, following the wise admonitions of the Emperor, continued to show a promising restraint in checking the impulse to attack which "the memory of Adowa" might have caused. The Italians began to suffer trouble with their communications and a pause of some weeks occurred. Short advances took place on the Somalia front in the south, and also from the southern corner of Eritrea, but were slow to develop further. Air bombing, however, began to produce some ominous symptoms of nerve-strain in the interior, despite the unfavourable conditions in which it had to operate—the wild nature of the country and the scattered population. The detachment of Dejasmatch Gugsa and other minor chiefs was a further symptom, and score, showing that the Italians were seeking to smooth the path of their strategy by fulfilling the old Roman maxim "divide and conquer".

Early in November the Italians resumed their southward advance, and on the 6th captured Makale, some eighty miles distant, again without meeting resistance. They then began to widen their penetration westward to the Takkaze River. If the Ethiopians were still showing a more than expected power to hold themselves in check, they had failed to develop real guerilla activity in harassing the advance. This was a lost opportunity, since the Italians suffered growing difficulties over the problem of supplying their forces. The scale of those forces accentuated the congestion of the inadequate communications. If the Ethiopians had been endowed with even a small air force they might at this time have precipitated an Italian disaster by attacking the narrow and scanty routes of supply on which the Italians depended. In the south General Graziani's forces captured Gorahai on the 5th, a coup in which they effectively used the "air barrage" method to overcome the defenders before the attack was launched. But the exploitation of this advance broke down, and the pursuing forces had to fall back.

Stagnation set in everywhere, and the initiative passed to the Ethiopians, who at last began to develop a modified form of guerilla counter-pressure. Circling round the Italians' far-extended flank, in mid-December—a few days after the Hoare-Laval proposals had been formulated—they regained the crossings of Takkaze by surprise and pushed some way towards Aksum. A week later Ras Seyyum recaptured part of the Tembien and thus began to threaten the Italians' hold on Makale. They have since admitted that the effect of these moves made their whole position precarious. The timely intervention of the Italian aircraft did much to curb the immediate danger, but the worrying pressure was renewed and extended.

Thus when the New Year opened, the Italians' military situation was not an enviable one. Contemplation of it led a large body of opinion in Europe to count on its becoming worse, and overlook the permanent elements of weakness which underlay the Ethiopians' situation. There was inadequate ground for such optimism so long as the Ethiopians lacked the means necessary for an intensive guerilla campaign, and until they also demonstrated their aptitude for it.

In mid-January the campaign took an ominous turn. Emboldened by Italian passivity, Ras Desta's forces pushed forward to the Somalian border near Dolo. If this was a potential threat to the flank of the Italian line of invasion from the south, it exposed the Ethiopians to a counter-stroke in an area where the terrain was favourable to tanks. General Graziani seized the opportunity, temporarily shifting his axis, and struck at the target thus offered. The tanks appeared in the Ethiopians' rear, their resistance collapsed, and the victory was followed up by a 240-mile pursuit to Neghelli. The following week the Italian forces in the north launched an offensive in the Tembien to relieve the pressure on the position at Makale. The Ethiopians met it with a counter-offensive in which partial success was purchased at heavy cost. It provided disquieting evidence of a new tendency —to make mass charges in face of machine-guns. The "memory of Adowa" was asserting itself, dangerously. The Ethiopians were blunting the edge of their own forces. Marshal Badoglio noted that after the failure of these repeated attacks the Ethiopians, "discouraged by their heavy losses, a shortage of ammunition, delay in the arrival of reinforcements and food supplies", had lapsed into a state of passivity. In consequence, he decided that he could safely take the offensive south of Makale, having now straightened out his communications.

Ras Mulugeta's forces awaited the assault and thereby exposed themselves to a concentrated artillery bombardment. After being blasted by high explosives, their position at Amba Aradam was encircled and overrun under cover of a thick fog—a fresh example of the benefit of the "attack in obscurity". By reckless counter-attacks the Ethiopian leaders had merely increased their losses and sapped the confidence of the men who were thus thrown against machine-guns. The Ethiopians lost some 20,000 men compared with 800 on the Italian side. Marshal Badoglio left the pursuit to his aircraft, and delivered a second stroke against the Ethiopian forces in the Tembien, followed by a third against the forces in Shire. As was inevitable, machine-power overcame an ill-equipped opponent who rashly accepted battle—and who each time did most of the attacking. Through this departure from common-sense strategy the Ethiopian forces had suffered a severe shaking, which was intensified by incessant air attacks. In following up their strokes the Italians made use of aircraft to overcome the brake of supply—the army corps on the right received its entire supplies by air in its advance to the Takkaze. By the beginning of March the Italian forces had regained the whole wedge of territory originally occupied in early November, and had extended it some twenty miles farther south, to Amba Alaji. This formidable position was abandoned by the Ethiopians without a fight. According to Italian accounts air action prevented the enemy's making a stand there, while Ethiopian accounts say that the position was handed over to the invaders by the arranged desertion of the Gallas and other tribes; the two accounts are not necessarily contradictory, for the causes may have been supplementary.

In his attacks Marshal Badoglio had profited by using wider tactical frontages, so that the enemy's attempted counter-moves were baffled and repelled by an extended fire-screen. The evidence of the enemy's discouragement also inspired him to widen his strategical front. A force from the southern corner of Eritrea advanced 120 miles across the Danakil desert and occupied the Aussa territory; its escorting aircraft fed it with supplies besides covering it against surprise. On the extreme western wing, near the Sudan border, other forces advanced across the Setit and pushed on south, towards Gondar. This important centre was captured by a motor column of 5000 men with 500 lorries, which, after a preliminary move of 150 miles through Eritrea territory, advanced 220 miles into enemy country in twelve days.

Even so, the Italians, in five months of war, had only covered a quarter of the way to Addis Ababa. More than

three hundred miles lay ahead, filled with great obstacles
of nature which had incalculable delaying power if they
were defended with resolution blended with discretion.
Although the ever-threatened advance on Harar succeeded, by its mere threat, in detaining in the south a
large proportion of the best-equipped Ethiopian forces,
the Emperor sent considerable reinforcements north to
make up the losses recently suffered, and he went up to
Lake Ashangi himself to take command. Thus, when
time and space factors were weighed, the chance of the
Italians reaching any decisive result before the rains
turned on the questions whether they could revolutionize the situation by some new means, or whether the
Ethiopians would commit fresh folly.

In March the Italians adopted the widespread use of
mustard gas, which they had shipped to Eritrea in large
quantities and had already tried occasionally in earlier
months. Naturally, they avoided using it in battle or laying it on their own direct line of advance, where it would
have been a hindrance to themselves; but there was
ample scope for its effective employment in covering
their flanks and communications against hostile counter-
moves, as well as in demoralizing the enemy's reserves
and his people behind the front. The effect of this new
weapon on a primitive race who had no protection was
dramatic—the nerve-shock being greater than the physical damage. It is worth recalling that when the Germans
first introduced gas into warfare, in April 1915, the
French African troops were completely demoralized,
streaming away in panic. Mustard gas naturally appears
to have magic proportions, since the victims may be

stricken without the slightest warning; merely through traversing a belt of ground which has been sprayed with the liquid some time earlier or through touching someone else who has a splash on his clothing. Although it is a disabling rather than a lethal weapon, and the deaths from it were relatively few in the European armies, the death-rate may be very high with unprotected troops and where no remedial treatment is available.

The rapid decline of Ethiopian morale which followed the repulse of their massed attacks and the advent of the gas campaign made it seem hopeless to await the Italians' advance or to rely on harassing operations against their flanks and communications. The Emperor was impelled to abandon wise strategy and adopt the desperate measure of launching his forces at the end of March to the assault of the Italian position at Mai Chio, south of Amba Alaji. The result was fatal, and could hardly have been otherwise. In their repeated attacks during the day of March 31st the Ethiopians had some 8000 men killed—more than a third of the attacking force. Next morning a fresh attack early was merely delivered to cover their retreat, which soon degenerated into a rout under the pressure of the air pursuit.

The collapse of this suicidal offensive was followed by the collapse of the Ethiopian army's will to resist. Thus the path of advance on Addis Ababa was suddenly cleared. There were many positions on the way where a comparatively small body of determined troops with machine-guns might have checked a multitude of assailants. But they were left open to the Italians, whose problem was now simplified, and reduced, to the organization of a triumphal march along a very rough road. This was largely a motorized march covered by a far-ranging barrage of aircraft.

On April 9th the Italians began their advance on Dessye, with the Eritrean army corps of some 18,000 men. It was fed mainly with supplies dropped by parachute during its march of 120 miles, covered in six days. Meantime Marshal Badoglio organized a force of 20,000 men, half Italians, half native troops, with a large convoy of lorries, to carry out the further advance on Addis Ababa. This picked force was brought up after the capture of Dessye and, leaving there on April 25th, it pressed forward in three columns by different routes, to reach Addis Ababa on May 5th. The invasion had been begun with a mass of over 300,000 men; the decisive advance, along the final three-quarters of the distance to the enemy's capital had been carried out by a severely pruned and newly proportioned spearhead composed of 20,000 men, some 2000 motor vehicles, and part of the 500 aircraft which had by now been concentrated in the war zone.

In the south Dedjasmatch Nasibu's army still offered a stout resistance on an entrenched line south of Sasa Baneh, showing the difference which even a trifle of modern equipment could make. Successive Italian attacks were repulsed for three days, but the lock was finally forced on April 18th with the aid of air bombardment. Graziani's advance was then again held up by the mud, and Sasa Baneh was not occupied until April 29th, after another stiff fight. With the Italians here on the offensive, the disparity of loss had been less marked than in the north; their casualties had been some 2000 compared with the Ethiopians' estimated 5000. But with the flight of the Emperor resistance had lost its point, while Nasibu's forces disintegrated under air pursuit once they were driven into the open. Thus the Italians' continued advance on Harar was a procession delayed only by the weather.

The machine had triumphed—over the man. The Lion of Judah had been crushed between the upper and nether jaws of Italy's mechanized forces. This reflection epitomizes the course of the Abyssinian war. It is no denial of the qualities of skill and courage which were called for, and displayed, in the handling of the modern weapons with which the Italian forces were equipped. There were stout-hearted men in the ranks of the invaders and in the command posts: without the power of resolution and endurance no deep advance into such a wild country would have been conceivable whatever the superiority of weapon-power. And back in Rome there was a human dynamo, charging the battery with an electric current. Yet when the fullest credit is given, apart from the moral issues, to these human factors, we are left with the basic fact that the decisive difference was produced by the war-machine.

The facts of the campaign point unmistakably to the conclusion that mechanization in the broad sense was the foundation on which the Italians' military superiority was built, while aircraft, the machine-gun, and mustard gas proved the decisive agents. The machine-gun on the ground for shattering the enemy's attacks, and the machine-gun in the air for exploiting its recoil. Mustard gas

as an invisible and disheartening screen against interference and also as a spreader of panic at a distance. Aircraft as a super-mobile cavalry arm, and as a means of
giving the ground forces a mobility, through elasticity of
supply, they could not otherwise have attained; also as a
distributor of disintegrating propaganda. If the Ethiopians played into the enemy's hands by providing him
with targets, it should also be realized that with the
advent of aircraft the chance of conducting successful
guerilla warfare has been much impaired, as was foreseen by that supreme exponent of the art, T. E. Lawrence. It counters the guerilla's mobility by superior
mobility. Yet, as it was, by trying to fight like an army
the Ethiopians gave the air arm its opportunity to show
its power in land warfare—for paralyzing the action, and
destroying the strength, of armies. It was thus a warning
to the armies of Europe, and to those who still place their
faith in mass of man-power.

18

Would Another War End Civilization?

THE QUESTION POSED IN THIS CHAPTER IS RE-
garded by many as being not even a question. Thus Mr.
A. A. Milne in his recent book, *Peace With Honour*,
which ably exposes so many irrational assumptions of the
past, says: "Is it not *absolutely* certain that another European war would mean the complete collapse of civilization?" Any qualifying effect of the question mark is
offset by the emphatic italics. And a little further on the
question mark even is dropped: "If we are on the eve of
another Armageddon, then we are on the eve of the
destruction of the world. That is absolutely certain."

Conscious of temerity in facing such certainty, I still
stick to my question mark. While recognizing the possibility that Mr. Milne's prediction may be justified, I can
see reasons why it may not. Even if it is fulfilled I am inclined to think that the effect will come in an indirect
and unexpected way rather than in the direct fashion
that most publicists suggest—that it will come through
the paralysis, not through the destruction, of civilization.

Here is the typical picture that the publicists paint.
There is striking agreement between them—is it perhaps

because, lacking time for prolonged research, they each copy one another? On the declaration of war, or anticipating it, the enemy's air-fleet appears over the capital. The city is deluged with bombs, usually poison gas bombs, and within a few hours it is a city of the dead. Millions have been suffocated. With certain variations of embroidery that pattern is continually repeated.

In *Cry Havoc* Mr. Beverley Nichols summons expert witnesses, apparently furnished by his news-clipping agency, to confirm the veracity of such a picture. Lord Halsbury is quoted as saying: "Mustard gas is the most deadly of known gases. In an area, say, Richmond to Barking, and from Finchley to Streatham (i.e. covering most of Greater London) an effective lethal dose would be only forty-two tons. In twelve hours every man, woman and child in that area might fail to live." Mr. Nichols adds in comment: "Since one R.A.F. bomber can now carry two tons of bombs, twenty planes could now do this work very easily." This sounds appalling, until one remembers that mustard gas proved the *least deadly* of gases in the last war, although the most widely disabling. The death-rate among casualties was less than four per cent. Its outstanding effectiveness lay not in killing, but in hindering and upsetting military plans—it was a first-class nuisance.

More weight attaches to the verdict of Thomas Edison, who is quoted as having said: "There is in existence no means of preventing an aeroplane flotilla from flying over London to-morrow and spreading over the millions of Londoners a gas which would asphyxiate these millions in a relatively short time. From twenty to fifty aeroplanes would be amply sufficient for the purpose . . . London's population could be choked to death in three hours."

A French physicist, Professor Langevin, is said to have stated: "A hundred aeroplanes, each carrying a ton of gas, could cover Paris with a gas cloud twenty metres thick. This could be done in an hour and if there were no wind Paris would be annihilated."

Even retired soldiers have voiced this view. Thus Lieut.-General von Altrock, of the German Army, has declared in the *Militar-Wöchenblatt:* "The population over a large area may expect destruction at any moment. The next war will take the form of mass murder of the civilian population rather than a conflict between armies."

Yet there are some notable witnesses who have ridiculed these alarming forecasts, and it is significant that they tend to be of higher scientific standing than the prophets of woe. Thus Dr. Freeth, who is chief research chemist of Imperial Chemical Industries, remarked at a meeting of the League of Nations Union that: "The amount of nonsense talked about poison gas is beyond belief." He pointed out that the most deadly gases could not be used in war—because of some simple catch. Carbon monoxide was one of the most dangerous. Every day omnibuses and cars were giving off large quantities. Yet, even when a mass of vehicles was held up in a narrow street, there were no casualties—because of the ventilating powers of the atmosphere. Carbon monoxide had a molecular weight of 30, while nitrogen had a molecular weight of 28 and oxygen of 32. "So if carbon monoxide were let loose, in a very short space of time it would be knocked about and dispersed by the molecules of the air which had, for practical purposes, the same molecular weight. That was why people are not killed in rows in Bond Street."

The first gas used in the war was chlorine: "its effect depended on perfect atmospheric conditions at the right moment", combined with an unsuspecting and therefore unprepared enemy. Once its surprise effect had passed its value was at an end.

"The really killing gases were light," Dr. Freeth emphasized, "and consequently easily dispersed by the molecular power of the atmosphere. All heavy gases were more or less immobile and could not move quickly. The only really useful military gas was mustard gas—and mustard gas was not a gas at all, but a heavy oil, made of alcohol, sulphur and chlorine." Owing to its prolonged effect it might dislocate traffic for several days until it had been dispersed. But it did not spread rapidly, and if it fell on wet porous soil it decomposed.

"Chemical warfare had got such a hold on the imagination of the civilian population that the main danger was psychological." The actual danger could be largely countered by precautions. "If in a gas raid a man could keep his head sufficiently to close the windows, put out the fire, and wait until the properly constituted authority had dispersed the gas, he would be reasonably safe. If he had no duty to perform, and simply got into a bath, smoked a pipe, and laughed, he would be practically completely safe!" Clearly, there was a whimsical touch in this last piece of advice, but it served to correct the other extreme of prognostication, and to emphasize that understanding is the best safeguard.

A broadly similar view has been expressed by Professor J. B. S. Haldane, although he has emphasized that the disabling potentialities of poisonous smokes as well as of mustard gas were not fully developed in the war. The reason is significant not only in its reflection on the military outlook but as a guide in speculation on the future. For Professor Haldane revealed in *Callinicus* that the use of mustard gas, which the Germans eventually introduced in 1917 (with most upsetting effect on the British Passchendaele offensive), was suggested by a British chemist to the military authority concerned with such questions. The General immediately asked "Does it kill?" He received the reply: "No, but it will disable enormous numbers of the enemy temporarily,"—whereat he said: "That is no good to us, we want something that will kill."

The trend of Professor Haldane's conclusions was that "if our anti-gas measures are sufficiently neglected, the consequences may be very serious". But he was as outspoken as Dr. Freeth in rejecting the alarming picture of "the wiping out of the population of whole cities" by gas bombardment.

Where experts differ it is difficult for the objective-minded enquirer, even though he be a student of war in general, to decide where the truth lies. But I have been impressed by the fact that the claims made for gas are least among the active chemists engaged in gas research whom I have met—their measure of unanimity is such that one might suspect that it was due to "trade-unionism" save for the fact that they agree, not in exaggerating, but in diminishing the importance of their own specialty.

What we can deduce, I think, from this controversy is that the vulnerability of the target counts for at least as much as the power of the weapon—and possibly counts for more. To that deduction, and its meaning, I shall return later.

But the feature which most strikes one in reading the forecasts of future horror, of cities blotted out in an hour, is the scant attention they pay to those who will direct the attacks—the military chiefs. By a curious self-contradiction, the very publicists who are most scornful of the military mind will take for granted that these air and gas attacks are directed with diabolical craft. They allow no credit to the profession of arms—not even the credit of having resisted throughout history every new development that has enhanced the terrible power of armed force. Yet they credit it with the overwhelmingly swift and decisive strokes of their imaginative picture.

It is left, however, to the General Staffs to conduct war—and their picture is very different to that drawn by the publicists. For the most part, it is still the picture of 1918 painted with the renewed confidence of 1914 upon a canvas of 1814. Right in the foreground stand the armies—not the air forces. As in 1914 the million-strong armies advance to battle—with each other. They are preceded by mechanized spearheads, but the bulk of the armies still march, partly through force of tradition, and partly because they are so large that mechanical transport only suffices to move their baggage and auxiliaries.

Their aim is the Napoleonic one of destroying the enemy's army, and their leaders cling to the dream of riding the whirlwind in Napoleonic style. They are still intoxicated by the offensive idea, for the sobering effect of the chilly blasts of 1914–1918 has been overcome by fresh draughts of pure martial spirit. The true soldier's thirst is unquenchable. Whatever disillusionment he meets, he is always sure that things will go right next time.

Certainly, in the background of his present picture some unpleasant spectres hover. Aircraft and tanks are among them. Gas and smoke, moreover, confuse the outline in a mildly disturbing way. It is admitted that all these newer elements may affect the issue, but they are primarily viewed as aids in destroying the enemy's army, and their possible inconvenience to one's own is shunned so far as possible, like other displeasing thoughts.

Thus there is ground for the assumption that however a next war may develop, the war plans at least may be on familiar lines, and the opening moves may be according to pattern—the pattern that past wars have traced. This may be no more than a continuation of what 1918 witnessed, or, at most, what 1919 held in store.

Such a view runs counter to a prevalent popular assertion—that every war is utterly different from the last. No fallacy is more confidently stated as fact—like all catchphrases this is hard to overtake once in its stride. Yet the truth is that history, even modern history, shows a gradual evolution in the character of wars. The paramount conditions of warfare in 1914 had governed the Russo-Japanese war a decade earlier, and had been clearly foreshadowed in the American Civil War half a century before.

This gradualness of evolution has owed much to the stout resistance which the military profession has always offered to novelty. The impetus of science in the nineteenth century did not suffice to storm these ramparts. The obstruction that the tank had to overcome on paper before it took the field in 1916 is well known; less familiar is the fact that it might have been available before the war began. There was Mr. de Mole's tank, superior in design to the one that was actually produced. But the design had been submitted to the War Office and was there pigeon-holed—until the war was over. There was also the promising idea contained in drawings submitted by a plumber of Nottingham. It also was unearthed after the war; the file bore the brief but decisive verdict: "The man's mad." Similar blindness marked the attitude of even the more thoughtful among leading soldiers to the possibilities of the air. When Foch watched the 1910 *Circuit de l'Est,* which proved the reliability of the new invention, he exclaimed: "That is good sport, but for the Army the aeroplane is no use."

A question that naturally arises to-day is whether the growth of dictatorship may overcome this resistance to novelty. A successful dictator is apt to be more of a realist than is the relatively cloistered member of a General Staff. Even if of military origin, he is less embedded in the professional grooves. By his circumstances, he is dealing every day in the fundamentals of strategy, instead of soaking in theory for most of a lifetime before he has a chance to practise against opponents. Also he is usually younger. A significant symptom is the marked increase of attention which has been given to military aviation and army mechanization in Italy since Mussolini, and in Germany since Hitler came to power. Under these dictators Balbo in the one country and Goering in the other have also been giving strategy a fresh direction—skywards. Here, certainly, is a warning of danger for democratic countries where military doctrines have been dictated by the heads of a professional class, autocratic within their own sphere and cut off from others.

Nevertheless, the case of Napoleon, the supreme example of military dictatorship, brings a measure of comfort. For with more power than any modern soldier has enjoyed, he made less use of it to develop new tactics and weapons. He was content to continue with the means that existed, merely developing their application. And even here it was mainly in imparting energy to a technique he had inherited that he excelled. Most astonishing of all incidents in his unevolving military career was his action in disbanding the French Balloon Corps, which in 1794 had made its first effective appearance in battle at Gosselies near Waterloo. If Napoleon had not stifled this promising infant, on its twenty-first birthday in June 1815 it might have saved him from irretrievable disaster at that very spot.

Appreciating the gradualness of military evolution, it behoves us to enquire as to the main lines it has taken in the past century or so.

First, was the growth of size. From France under the Revolution and Napoleon, through America in the Civil

War and Prussia under Moltke, the armies swelled to the millions of 1914. Yet back in the eighteenth century Marshal Saxe had foreseen the hindrances of size when he delivered his dictum: "Multitudes serve only to perplex and embarrass."

Second, came the growth of fire-power, beginning with the adoption of rifles and breech-loading weapons. This, imposed on size, conduced to a growing paralysis of warfare on land and sea.

Third was the growth of industrialization. The change from well-distributed agricultural communities to a concentration of population and an interdependence of areas, together with the more complex needs of such a civilization, gave more influence in war to economic objectives. By acting against those, even in the comparatively primitive South, Sherman decided the issue of the American Civil War. Soldiers in Europe, however, remained unable to see much beyond the opposing army. Their eyes were bloodshot. Yet in the end it was the economic pressure, mainly applied by the Navy, which decided the issue of the World War.

A fourth was the revolutionary growth of mobility, due in turn to the steam engine and the motor. Paradoxically, its chief effect when added to the other tendencies was to reduce the effective mobility of armies. The railway—which had speed but not flexibility, the other constituent of mobility—fostered the accumulation of masses, and these were hampered not only by their own bulk but by the growth of fire. The road-motor, a much later development, was neglected until the war came and was then at first applied merely to the service

of mass. Not until it was embodied in the tank did it
begin to assist the recovery of mobility—by making it
possible for men to advance in face of bullets. The aeroplane likewise began as a mere auxiliary, and to this
minor role it was still mainly confined as its numbers
grew. Even in the greatest bombing raid on London
only thirty-three machines were employed, although
four thousand were in use for the narrower duties of
army co-operation. But in the last phase of the war, aircraft showed their powers at the expense of armies by
frustrating the escape of the defeated Bulgarian, Turkish
and Austrian armies: they turned the ebbing tide into a
stagnant shambles.

What were the outstanding lessons of the war along
these lines of evolution? The first, certainly, was that
the huge conscript armies tended to make war inevitable,
just as, when war was engaged, they tended to make it
immobile. "Mobilization means war," the German am-
bassador threateningly said to the Russian Foreign Minister with more profound truth than he intended. For,
once the mass of the people were summoned to arms
from their normal occupation, an atmosphere was created
in which peace-feelers were stifled. Moreover, these
armies were so cumbrous, their movement so complex,
that even direction could not be modified. Thus, when
the Kaiser, clutching at a report that France might for-
sake Russia's side and remain neutral, said to Moltke, the
Chief of the German General Staff: "We march, then,
only towards the East?" Moltke replied that this was
"impossible. The advance of armies formed of millions
of men was the result of years of intricate work. Once

planned it could not possibly be changed." Even when a twenty-four hour delay of the invasion of France was ordered, Moltke pathetically recorded: "It was a great shock to me, as though something had struck at my heart." So the millions went forward.

But when they reached the battlefield, they were stopped by the machine-guns, few as these were. Back in 1884, a military prophet had acclaimed the machine-gun as "concentrated essence of infantry". Military authorities had paid little attention to such prophecies—until the war came in 1914. Then it was shown that one man sitting behind a machine-gun was equal to ten, a hundred, even a thousand, who were rushing on him with the bayonet. The generals were puzzled. They had always counted strength by count of heads.

It was the machine-gun that made infantry advance hopeless and cavalry futile. The next four years were spent in trying to overcome this obstacle.

First, the generals, true to their theory of mass, tried masses of artillery. This method achieved poor results in proportion to the effort. It made a short advance possible but forbade a long one—by ploughing up the ground over which the advance had to be made.

A new method dawned in 1916—the use of tanks. Reluctantly accepted by authority, it did not receive a real opportunity in the field until the last year. Then it produced longer and quicker advances than had hitherto been made, and proved, by German confession, the decisive weapon. If the war had continued into 1919, the Allies, at a young colonel's instigation, were going to try a more original way of using tanks—to pass straight through the front, neglecting the enemy's fighting men, and strike direct at his headquarters and communication centres, dislocating his fighting power at the source.

The Germans had also tried, in 1915, a new means to overcome the barrier. This was gas. Luckily for the Allies, the German soldiers thwarted the German chemists, and the best chance of a decisive result was forfeited. Still, by ringing the changes on various types, gas continued to play an important part. The most effective, by far, was mustard gas, which disabled by blistering the skin and took effect even after a long interval. The strategic effect, however, was more in hampering an enemy's attack than in assisting one's own. Thus it tended to increase the paralysis in which the war was already gripped.

One possibility of overcoming machine-guns was largely neglected—the advance in obscurity. Night attacks were rare, for fear of confusion—although this was a lesser risk than a daylight advance in face of defending machine-guns. Smoke screens were never fully developed. When first suggested in 1914, Kitchener had emphatically declared that they "would be of no use for land operations"! Yet in 1918, it was under cover of fog—nature's smoke—that the Germans repeatedly broke through the Allied front. When fog was lacking, they failed. It is strange that neither side sought to produce artificial fog on a great scale.

At sea likewise the same lines of evolution led to the same conclusion—a state of general paralysis. The traditional purpose of destroying the enemy's main forces in battle was never fulfilled, and although the fleets were once within range of each other, at Jutland, analysis of that tactically ineffective encounter tends to emphasize the factors that made for paralysis.

Naval development had been marked by swelling as on land, although this elephantiasis at sea affected the size of individual ships rather than the numbers of a fleet. Battleships became so large, and hence so few compared with Nelson's day, that admirals became more reluctant to risk them. And the growth of fire-power tended to keep the fleets apart; fighting at long ranges made a decision more difficult. To this check was added that of a new weapon, the torpedo; if it did not attain the results in sea fighting that had been anticipated by the prophets, this was largely because the fear of it made the admirals shy of pursuing an offensive movement—and thereby exposed the ineffectiveness of a battle-fleet. The lighter craft, too, were in consequence diverted to the unprofitable duty of chaperoning their big sisters. The British official history candidly confesses: "The Grand Fleet could only put to sea with an escort of nearly one hundred destroyers . . . the German U-boats had hampered our squadrons to an extent which the most expert and far-sighted naval officer had never foreseen." A few months after the "victory" of Jutland, the danger of a German invasion of Denmark loomed on the horizon of the British Government; after examination by the Admiralty, the conclusion was reached that "for naval reasons it would be almost impossible to support the Danes at all". What a humiliating confession of impotence! The shadow of the German submarine was longer than the shadow of Nelson's column.

Nor was that all. The growth of industrialization had made nations, Britain above all, more dependent on overseas supply. By multiplying commerce it had multiplied the targets for indirect attack. While British destroyers were chaperoning battleships, the German submarines were sinking British mercantile shipping—until Britain herself was in sight of collapse. When part of the destroyers were diverted to protect commerce, the Grand Fleet had to be practically locked up for its own safety! It was history's most ironical case of "protective arrest".

As for the growth of mobility, through the suppression of sails by steam, its influence is to be traced throughout the stalemate that prevailed. Its effect, as on land, was to engender a fundamental immobility. In the case of the outer and greater naval power this prevented it destroying the enemy's fleet; in the case of the inner and weaker, Germany, it ensured her ultimate collapse from pernicious anæmia.

Here we have traced the evolution of the past that has produced the present state of warfare. What of the future? Unless the whole current of history be reversed, it will be a prolongation of the past. It is not practical to deal here with hypothetical influences that might revolutionize the situation. Electric waves and stratospheric rockets may be left to the imaginative novelist until the scientist has produced results that not only stand inspection but provide ground for scientific military speculation. Meantime, we shall be wise to bear in mind that the pigeonholes of War Offices have proved an effective antidote to any new poison—at least until its greatest menace has passed.

So, on the basis of what exists and what reflection shows, let us try to trace-the outline of another great war —the outline of the opening act, at least. And for reasons better or worse, there may be no second act in the true sense; only an epilogue.

By the very force of custom, and the natural desire to justify their existence, it is likely that the armies may again attempt to act as they did in 1914. We may even see the many-headed columns of troops passing down the roads across the frontier. But it needs no small feat of imagination to see them going very far. They may be able to start if they get off before the starter's pistol as in 1914, and make their approach marches under cover of night; it is likely that the major part of the opponent's air force will be aiming at more important targets during this initial phase. But once across the frontier, they will meet brakes more severe than any in past experience. Chains of machine-guns ensconced in hidden concrete casemates or rushed up in motor vehicles; a cloud of tanks looming on their flanks; a darker cloud of aircraft overhead that will force them to disperse, besides assailing the long supply trains that cannot disperse. There has also been much progress since the last war in the art of stopping progress by demolitions. An invasion may soon become slow motion, and then a pitiful stagnation.

Motor vehicles abound not only in the establishment of armies but in the households of every town and village. Motor vehicles, even the humblest runabouts, can carry machine-guns; and machine-guns are movement-stoppers. They can be switched to any point, to block any threatening line of invasion, and will certainly impede the enemy's advance. By use of the motor, armed civilians may play a more formidable part in the future than ever in the past, while professional motor bandits may turn temporarily to patriotic employment like the freebooters of old.

If and when the opposing armies come in contact, the machine-gun obstacle, intensified by wire entanglements and land minefields, will still have to be overcome. Is there any more chance of success than in the last war? The contrary, rather. For the proportion of machine-gun-destroying weapons—artillery and tanks—is at present lower in all armies than it was in 1918. And, on the other hand, the proportion of machine-guns, heavy and light, has greatly increased. Thus, it is a matter of simple arithmetic to deduce that the advantage of the defensive is even greater than before. Realizing this, a clear-sighted commander-in-chief may elect to stay on the defensive and await his enemy's attack. His troops will thus suffer less physical damage and less shock to their confidence, but they will not achieve any positive result unless the enemy is rash enough to persist so long in his vain attempt to advance that he exhausts his troops so severely that they cannot withstand an attack in their turn. Another possibility is that both sides will be clear-sighted, and await attack—in which case they will merely produce stalemate without conflict.

If mustard gas be employed, early stalemate is still more probable. For an army will tend to spray mustard gas along the parts of its front where it intends to stay on the defensive, and to concentrate its forces on the parts more favourable for its own attack. As the favourable

and unfavourable sectors will commonly be the opposite
for the enemy army, we may even see a reduction to
absurdity by which each army's would-be offensive sector is blocked by the enemy's mustard gas barrier—so
that the two will sit facing each other helplessly, separated by a continuous mutual barrier which both have
combined to raise!

Tanks offer a possible means of advance, both in face
of machine-guns and across a gas-belt. But the proportion of them is so small, and the fear of them so great,
that each side is likely to give its first attention to blocking and destroying the other's tank forces. So long as the
tank forces are but a small fraction of the total forces,
this effort at cancellation has the chances in its favour.
Moreover, until it does, the fear of the enemy's armoured
troops will have a numbing effect on the movement of
all unarmoured troops—and thus promise to aggravate
the paralysis of the past.

The prospect for armies is a dull one. The gloomiest
aspect is due to the cloud overhead. Air attack is not
much of a menace to infantry who are deployed or entrenched. But long columns on the march are vulnerable.
Their movement can easily be·stopped—and if they cannot move they cannot reach the battlefield. Tanks and
other cross-country vehicles, by contrast, offer a poor
target to air bombers while on the move, especially when
they move off the roads on a wide front. When they
halt, voluntarily or involuntarily, they become vulnerable. Moreover, they are dependent, like all troops, on
being supplied with fuel, food and ammunition. It is
against the long and narrow arteries, as well as the con-

centrated sources of supply, that air attack has its greatest scope. There is no need to accept all the claims made by air enthusiasts for the present accuracy of bomb-dropping. The system of supply of a great army is so complex that it can easily be thrown out of gear. Dislocation will suffice, with little destruction, to cripple the power of movement. Every increase in the mobility—the speed and range—of aircraft threatens to increase the immobility of armies.

Thus the awe-inspiring advance of the armies may end in a general farce—although locally it may spell tragedy. For little imagination is needed to picture the mobs of unfed soldiery, breaking their ranks as hunger becomes acute and pillaging their own towns and countryside—to the quicker starvation of all in common, unless an armistice be speedily arranged so that communications may be restored. And the war may peter out in an atmosphere charged with the sense of futility.

A further deduction is unmistakable. The larger the army that a country maintains and tries to mobilize on the outbreak of war, the weaker that country may be. For, by the congestion of all the national arteries that large-scale mobilization entails, it will immensely increase its own difficulties and dangers in face of air attack, thus diminishing its own ability to withstand the sudden stresses of the first days of war.

It is possible that a would-be aggressor might be deterred by foresight from these old methods of invasion—although there is only a glimmer of the new idea in the present composition of the European armies. An inroad of mechanized forces, powerful but relatively small,

would certainly be more difficult to check than the advance of marching millions—especially if it came without
warning. Such a force might assemble many miles behind
the frontier overnight and be across before morning. It
might overwhelm the defender's frontier-covering troops
before they realized that war had broken out, and pierce
by surprise a chain of forts. The possibility might be the
greater if such a stroke were launched by machines
equipped with direction-finders under cover of artificial
fog—this is a potential development which deserves serious attention.

But even if successful, it is difficult to picture these
forces achieving more than to multiply the disorder in
the interior of the country which would already have
been created by air attack on the industrial centres and
arteries of traffic. Unless the defender signified his immediate surrender, and this would be difficult for him in
a state of chaos, it would be necessary to follow up the
stroke with reinforcements and occupying troops. Here
would lie the invader's hardest problem—harder than
ever in the past, since the difficulty of maintaining communications is greater. It is conceivable that by extraordinary foresight, by gauging the trend of developments
exactly, and by perfectly calculated measures to diminish
his own vulnerability while maintaining his strength, an
attacker might succeed in producing the internal collapse
of his ·adversary without courting his own—but such
foresight has never been shown by any makers of war.
The greater probability is that the sequel to the attack
would be a mutual breakdown on land.

At sea, a similar prospect prevails. To the paralytic

power which the submarine exercised in 1914–1918, is now added the power of the faster surface light-craft, the new torpedo-armed 60 m.p.h. speedboat, and of the 200 m.p.h. aircraft—soon, by all signs, to be 300 m.p.h. even for a normal service machine. Here again, the effect can be measured without counting upon the possibility that the battle-fleets may be bombed out of existence. For practical effect, paralysis will suffice, without destruction. And when we reckon the new agents now added to the submarine, it needs a greater stretch of the imagination to see·the battle-fleets being less paralyzed than they were in 1914–1918 than to see them recovering their lost powers under greater impediments. The stagnation of the trade-routes, now that they are exposed over so many miles to attack from shore-based aircraft, is equally calculable. If the flow of commerce could barely continue under the pressure of a few score submarines, themselves slow and vulnerable, is it reasonable to assume that it can survive this multiplied menace of to-day and to-morrow?

Nations may still go to war in face of the warning. But can they go on with it? The outcome seems more likely to be merely ridiculous than to be fatally decisive. Certainly, so far as the conflict of armed forces is concerned.

This reflection, however, does not banish the risk to the nations who go to war. That danger is two-fold; first, that they will not come to their senses in time to retrieve order from the chaos into which their communications will be plunged; second, that irreparable damage may be done by deliberate attack on the centres of population, ignoring the opponents' armed forces.

There is an almost universal assumption that any future war will open with a concentrated air attack on the enemy's capital. I see reasons, and have already indicated some, for doubting this popular certainty.

We should be rash to place unreserved trust in "rules of war". Recent history shows all too clearly that rules are broken as soon as they are felt as an endangering hindrance to a nation that thinks it is fighting for its life—a conviction that has taken root with the growth of "democracy". But it would be equally unhistorical to disregard altogether the restraining power of such rules —especially in the early stages of a war, before frustration or disaster had come to aggravate the sense of constraint.

It is more probable that direct injury to the population will come indirectly, through attack on military objectives—such as arsenals, aerodromes, and dockyards— which lie in a thickly populated area. The intermixture favours the least scrupulous combatant by offering him a good opportunity and excuse for achieving a coincident effect on the enemy people's will. The use of incendiary mingled with high-explosive bombs—a combination that is likely to be more effective and militarily economic than gas—will have more promise at such objectives of striking inflammable targets and thus spreading a conflagration outwards. Such fires, in turn, are likely to spread panic faster and wider than by the destruction of comparatively isolated blocks of houses and business offices

attained in the promiscuous bombing of a city. This possibility emphasizes the importance of separating military
from civil objectives as far as possible, by removing
munition works and other military establishments away
from the cities.

I have already referred to the antidote which is latent
in War Offices. So long as the official military minds of
the world cling to the dogmas of Clausewitz, that the
main aim in war is the destruction of the enemy's armed
forces, so long may we count on the restraining power of
a military "rule of war" that is far more potent than any
of the rules drawn up at Geneva. Professional indoctrina-
tion goes deeper than humanitarianism. Moreover, although the war-minded statesman may be free from this
professional bias towards battle, he will be influenced by
his responsibility to the people in his cities, and perhaps
also by his own presence among them. Fear of instant
reprisals—all the stronger from being in this new case a
fear of the unknown—may well incline him to accept the
inherent military preference for an orthodox war-plan,
aimed mainly at the enemy's forces and their bases.

Another influence, working to the same effect, is the
irrepressible optimism of the military mind. To the scientific historian the way that the wish has fathered the
thought throughout the course of warfare, and led to
endless futilities, is apt to seem the most extraordinary of
military phenomena. Yet it must be realized that the
power of command is largely based on this confidence,
however often misplaced. Inherent in the military nature,
it has now recovered from the shocks of hard experience
in 1914–1918, which were the less severely felt because

of the resiliency of this optimism. Studying the military leaders of the various powers in Europe to-day, one finds that with rare exceptions they are inflated anew with the confidence in victory that their predecessors had in 1914. They are dreaming again of an irresistible offensive and of a rapid decision. Only a short time ago the Italian authorities exuberantly declared that "trench-warfare was obsolete"—that "the first onslaught of tanks and fast-moving detachments would break through trench-lines, force fighting into the open, and make movement so rapid that nothing would be gained by digging new trenches". And the authorities of other armies echoed the opinion. To a cool observer it seemed the more curious since Italy, while admirably endowed with natural defences against an invader, is even more deficient in tanks for attack than some of the other countries.

If this soldierly optimism unhappily makes for war, by its tendency to delude governments as to the chances, it promises a compensation—that it will direct the initial war-effort along the customary military road, which appears to be a cul-de-sac. As the martial crowds pour down it, congestion and then stagnation are likely to come as soon as air attack on the communications takes effect. The armies may not even reach the battlefield before paralysis overtakes them from the tail up.

It is then that the danger of direct air attack on the cities may come to a head. The air forces, with the military side of their mission accomplished, may be concentrated on the civil. But modern air forces depend on a large ground organization, and this may hardly escape the prevailing chaos. Thus the air menace may be limited, if not crippled, at source—just when the menace would otherwise reach its peak.

Against a limited menace, adequate preparation for protection is possible—not so much by direct defence as by diminishing vulnerability. For this it is an urgent necessity to remove military targets from the neighbourhood of cities, and more feasible than the construction of innumerable shelters. Air raid precautions and emergency preparations of all kinds, will count for much. But of all the possible safeguards, education and understanding are likely to prove the greatest. And on these equally depends the answer to the question whether a state is prepared, mentally as well as practically, to cope with the state of chaos that war promises to produce at an early stage. The fate of the peoples is thus to a large extent in their own hands.

"If you wish for peace, prepare for war," ran the old Roman maxim. It is still true, but in a different sense. The wiser course to-day is not to multiply forces, especially the massive type of forces that conduce to the chaos of communications, but to prepare indirect protection by diminishing the target and inoculating the system against susceptibility to chaos. True preparedness lies in understanding the trend of modern war.

The most reassuring symptom is, certainly, that the most military-minded peoples at present show a misunderstanding of modern war. The proof lies in their retention of huge conscript armies that must inevitably hamper their power of adaptability to modern war conditions. Fatness is not strength. It is clear that they have missed the meaning of mobility. This is natural. For thousands of years war has been waged at 3 m.p.h. In a generation we have sprung to the possibility of waging it at 300 m.p.h. Such a change baffles military comprehension. So the military-minded peoples strive to achieve the impossible feat of blending 3 m.p.h. forces with 300 m.p.h. The proverbial folly of putting new wine into old skins is nothing compared with that of putting aviation spirit into inflammable skins. Happily, the risk is greatest for the men who make the unthinking experiment. Thereby there is reasonable hope that another war may produce the collapse of the attack before the collapse of civilization. And that a sense of the ridiculous may bring the warring peoples to their senses before they can renew the war-effort.

Index

GENERAL

Abyssinian War, 29, 51-3, 88, 117, 174, 238ff.
Addis Ababa, 242, 252
Adowa, battle of, 240, 246, 249
Alexander the Great, 35, 177
Amba Aradam, battle of, 53, 249
American Civil War, 158, 200, 226, 227, 263, 264-5
Arab Revolt, the, 241

Badoglio, Marshal, 249, 250, 253
Balbo, Marshal, 264
Baldwin, Rt. Hon. Stanley, 83
Balearic Isles, 127
Belgium, 143, 144
Belisarius, 35
Bismarck, 219
Bloch, M., 210
Blomberg, Field Marshal von, 38
Boer War, 200, 227
Bombay, 131
Bourcet, Pierre de, 56
Britain, policy, 13, 15, 18, 20, 116ff.
— air, 27, 81, 83, 84, 86, 88, 89, 92, 121
— army, 73ff., 82, 84, 86, 89, 93, 164
— navy, 83, 84, 87, 88, 92, 118ff., 164

Cæsar, Julius, 161, 177
Canary Isles, 127
Cape of Good Hope, route by, 120, 127, 131, 133
Chetwode, Field-Marshal Sir Philip, 208
Clausewitz, Carl von, 34, 218-21, 228, 278
Clive, 35
Colin, General, 57
Cortés, 35
Crete, 126
Cromwell, 177
Cyprus, 128, 129

Danton, 142
De Lesseps, Ferdinand, 122
De Mole, Mr., 263
Denmark, 269
Disraeli, Benjamin, 123, 128
Dodecanese, 29, 126, 128, 130
Dolo, 248

Edison, Thomas, 257
Egypt, 88, 122, 129

Foch, Marshal, 200, 208, 209, 263
France, policy, 30, 83, 117ff.
— air, 28, 83, 86
— army, 55ff.
Franco, General, 127

SPECIAL FACTORS